TRANSFORMING THE RELATIONSHIP

JOSIAH & JAMES H JOHNSON

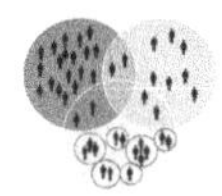

TRANSFORMING THE RELATIONSHIP

CONTENTS

Foreword

In the fall of 2019, my father faced his retirement creeping up on him. Though he had already deferred his social security, pension, and socialized a succession plan, it didn't feel like it would become a reality. It was in that void that I noticed a spark of "unfinished business" in how he talked about retirement. He wanted to achieve more before that time came. It wasn't in greater professional aspirations, but his spark came from a desire to pass down his gifts and insights to the larger market. Often during my coffee chats with my father, the salesman since he was 12 or so, sounded less enthusiastic about the sales leads or the sales process itself, and more eager about the social dynamics at play. As his professional career ended, he worked to identify the key factors that had led him to have success. The simple theme that seemed to rise to the top and was common to all his sales was simple; develop relationships. To better understand his view on relationships, it helps to know my father. I'll let him tell his story:

James Johnson>> *First off, I must admit that I am a member of the baby-boomer generation. I grew up in a small town of five thousand, 60 miles west of Minneapolis, MN. I was blessed to be the baby of the family and inherited a brother and two sisters and parents who loved us very much. My father was a WWII Marine veteran survivor, and my mother was a hard-working stay-at-home mom until I was in 6th grade, when she went to work for our family to provide medical insurance. I did not grow up "entitled" to anything other than the love of my parents, discipline when my behavior was unacceptable, and equitable compensation in return for whatever job I completed.*

I started to work in my father's furniture store when I was strong enough to carry furniture and use the tools to help him install carpet. I also had several paper routes and would often obtain my Christmas gifts for the family by selling newspaper subscriptions. I set out on my first paying *job at Sam's Supermarket when I was 12 and worked on and off there for 10 years starting at $0.25 per hour. I was taught how to sweep floors, stock shelves, cut meat, drive the home delivery truck (after I acquired a driver's license) and listen to and care for our customers. Looking back, every job I had involved people and relationships. It did not matter whether I was delivering papers or groceries, making or fulfilling promises for quality products or delivering services that had to be provided.*

College graduation afforded me a BA in Philosophy at Crown College which I quickly utilized by returning to my father's carpet business. I may not have been able to apply my "book knowledge" to the business, but it's where I felt called. I enjoyed the craft and the process of the business but what I cherished and valued even more was working with my father and developing a mature relationship.

*At that time, my vision of the future would be to develop and expand my father's carpet and flooring business. That was until one snowy February day when a local businessperson approached me at the Colonial café and asked me to come and work with him in his egg and feed business as a marketing/salesman. I told him that I knew little about eggs, chickens or feed. He replied that he would teach me about the product, but the ability to develop relationships with people was an asset that I possessed that could not be <u>taught</u> but had to be **caught**. He said that over the years he had observed my work ethic and personality, and now wanted me to come and work with him. The man was Robert Sparboe and my relationship with Bob would shape my future relative to my desire to be in business and work in corporate America. I learned many valuable lessons while working with Bob, lessons that shaped these past 41 years in the insurance industry.*

I was a philosophy major in college, not a business or marketing major, so my perspectives at times may be based more on revelation and the resultant feelings rather than on the logic acquired through market research.

I'm not apologizing, just merely stating the soon to be demonstrated opinion; if someone doesn't sell a car there, is no need to worry about the design, engineering or the manufacturing process.

For there to be a dimes worth of profit for selling an item, there must be a seller, and a buyer. It's the simple law of economics.

The material in this book describes how two or more concepts, people or objects are connected and stay connected. Man was born in relationship and unfortunately man may choose to die alone outside of relationship, self-isolated in a society where social media has minimized involvement and concern, text messages are substituted for phone calls, and digital meetings for a Sunday afternoon trip to visit the family.

It was my father's background and vision that served as the catalyst for this book. Our countless conversations during coffee breaks, lunches, and golf sessions have instilled in me the same fervor to combine his experiences and wisdom with my own and offer them to anyone willing to listen.

Relationships have also served as a defining aspect in most of my life decisions as well. A respected teacher influenced my pursuit in an engineering degree. My best friend guided me in the selection of undergrad studies. A guest at a hotel I was working at offered me a chance to grow in my young career as an Engineer.

My early years in manufacturing held immense value for me. While some professionals spend their entire careers in manufacturing encountering a few large-scale changes, I was fortunate to lead and implement over 20 such changes over six years. In that first half-decade of work I nurtured my passion for further business education and obtained my MBA through the University of Minnesota – Duluth. A series of shifts at the manufacturing plant eventually led me to relocate across the US to Mobile, AL, for a new position. This leap later resulted in my present role as a consultant. Over the past five years, I've had the privilege to work alongside a dynamic team that engages with companies in various stages of business performance (struggling or growing) that strive to optimize their financial performance.

Through our collective careers and personal experiences, both my father and I can attribute a great deal of our progression and opportunities to a select group of relationships that God has placed into our lives. We are profoundly grateful for understanding that these individuals were strategically placed in our lives for specific moments. Many of these relationships have propelled me to the "next" stage of my life, while others have remained constants, accompanying us on this journey.

My father and I have long held the ambition of jointly embarking on a project that would serve others well. While we mulled over starting our own consulting business, it wasn't practical at that juncture due to our separate life circumstances. There was also talk of me taking over his client base in life insurance, but my interests did not align with sales in that sector. It seemed for some time like our opportunity for a joint venture had slipped by until the concept for this book came to light—a project where we could work together on a story yet to be completed. We began this endeavor with enthusiasm and the anticipation that it would provide both enjoyment and value to you as the reader.

Introduction

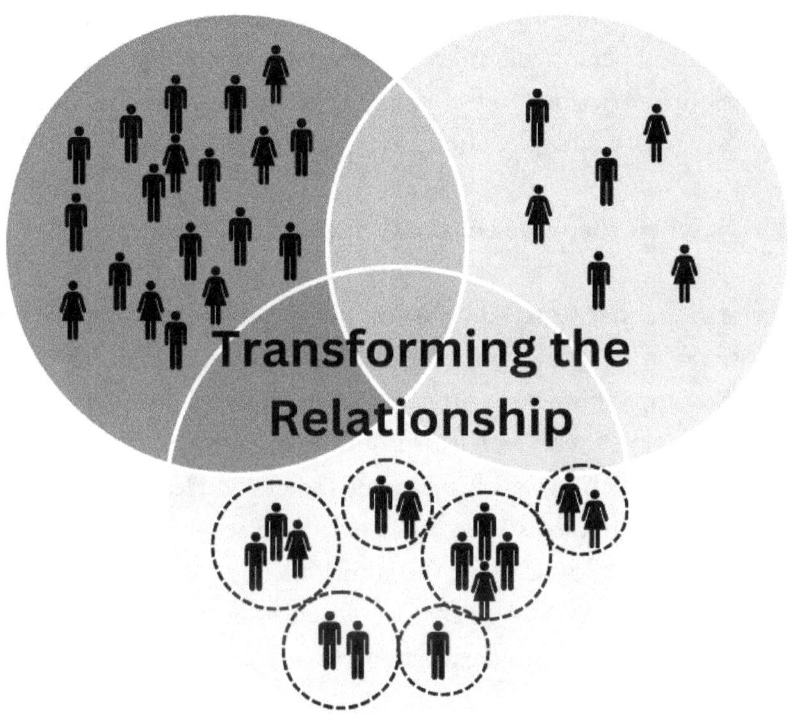

Connectedness vs. Relationship

The Covid-19 pandemic, with its enforced quarantines, taught me a crucial lesson: being connected isn't the same as having meaningful relationships. In today's digital era, establishing connections can be as quick and superficial as fulfilling certain search criteria and hitting the "follow" button. This action latches you onto the digital presence of someone else almost instantly, allowing for a peek into their existence, while they sometimes get to peek into yours. Such is the modern apex of digital connection.

Connectedness is undoubtedly valuable. It offers us the ability to interact with others with minimal effort and experience immediate gratification when we seek to engage. During the pandemic, connectedness was our lifeline to the world outside the confines of our homes, especially for critical personnel (a heartfelt thank you to them). It provided a way for our restrictions to feel less confined and allowed us to engage with a wide array of people, but....

That's when the wide chasm 1st appeared to me.

It was in the first 48 to 72 hours of one of those quarantine that the true distinction between connectedness and genuine relationships became starkly apparent. Even with the transparent walls created by digital interactions, connectedness felt profoundly isolating and lonely. While many of the interactions, such as sharing memes and leaving comments, occurred with individuals with whom we have some form of relationship, these actions didn't bridge the emotional gap.

What I yearned for was a sense of closeness or bond with people. I missed the small talk about weather and sports, or latest celebrity activities.

I longed for the everyday exchanges at the local grocery store to regain their normalcy. I wanted the small-business owner to entice me to buy more products rather than to maintain a 6-foot distance. I craved the water-cooler chats with colleagues and despised how even the most well-intentioned virtual meetings or "social hours" always seemed to carry an air of formality no matter how hard we tried to make them feel casual and natural.

Yes, I was connected, but I didn't experience the true depth of relationships.

It's not my intention to rekindle how we felt in isolation, so this may be one of the few instances where I discuss Covid-19 in this book. Rather, my hope is that as you read these pages, you might consider how these insights could apply to the relationships we were and may remain digitally connected to today!

CHAPTER 1

3 Categories of Relationships

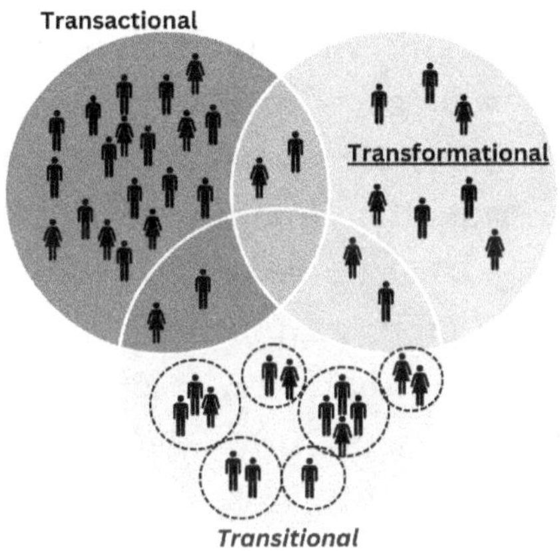

My father and I hold the view that relationships are fundamental to our existence, influencing our experiences, emotions, and life paths. Relationships, or rather the connections and bonds built through shared experiences, emotions, and interactions amongst individuals, represent deeply personal and distinct ties that are uniquely meaningful to each of us yet may defy precise assessment. At times we neglect to analyze these bonds for lack of time or effort, or simply because it feels like a dull task.

My oldest daughter viewed my writings on this topic as less captivating than the fiction she enjoys. I respect her viewpoint, but I am eager to pass on a lesson that my father taught me from a young age—a lesson spanning over twenty years—on the importance of understanding and defining the different relationships we establish. He believed it was an essential topic to explore in writing. My father, who worked as a commissioned salesman for forty years, always said that relationships were more influential to his success than the actual products. Similarly, during my ten years in the manufacturing sector, I recognized that despite having knowledge and expertise from my education, fostering good relationships with colleagues was indispensable for professional success.

For a relationship to thrive, it requires effort and commitment from both parties and a willingness to listen, *understand*, and compromise. We found the level of *understanding* to be one of the key traits that segments our relationships into the different categories that we'll dive into in this book. Shankar Vedantam, founder of Hidden Brain Media, a company that produces media to help curious people understand the world, and themselves, recently produced a podcast episode on "What Makes Relationships Thrive". Below are key principles from his discussion with Harry Reis, a Professor of Psychology at University of Rochester, who studies the factors that influence the quantity and closeness of social interaction, and the consequences of different patterns of socializing for health and psychological well-being:

Understanding is one of the most important things that we want in our close relationships, and it is essential for things like love, trust, and caring to work. "One of the most powerful things that we desire is for there to be real understanding in those relationships. That the people on the other side know who we are and are caring and validating and accepting of that person."

If the understanding of us is different than how we understand ourselves, we may feel inauthentic, unrewarding, or like an imposter. "If your understanding of me is different than how I understand myself, then when you tell me how much you love me, you're telling me that you love somebody different than me."

Understanding is not only important in intimate relationships, but also in professional relationships, such as in academia, medicine, and education. "In the academy, it's very important that our colleagues, the people who we're working with toward the common goal of doing research and educating students and each other, it's very important that they understand what we are trying to do in our work."

Feeling misunderstood is a growing problem in the modern world, where we encounter more people from different backgrounds, goals, and contexts. "People feeling misunderstood is something that is growing by leaps and bounds in the world we live in now. With all these stresses and tensions that we have, there's more and more of a need to get connected with other people and part of that connection involves the sense of really understanding where people are coming from."

Understanding may vary in depth depending on the category of relationship, but it is necessary to produce the greatest benefit. So how many relationships will we have to understand and evaluate in our life? Well according to a study conducted by the University of Kansas in 2010, the average American has about **610** ties, or relationships, throughout their lifetime. This includes both close relationships and more distant acquaintances. We can debate on what that number may be, but a fact is that each of those interactions is as unique as the people participating in them.

The different categories that we'll help provide definition and examples of in this book are: **Transactional, Transitional and Transformational.**

Transactional: Relationships that occupy the "customer service" aspect of an interaction, where both parties aim to benefit from a positive outcome.

Transitional: Relationships that are typically not selected by ourselves, but rather the environment we find ourselves in for a period of time.

Transformational: Relationships that are born when we help another become someone they never could have become without our interaction, and we become someone that we never would have become without their investment.

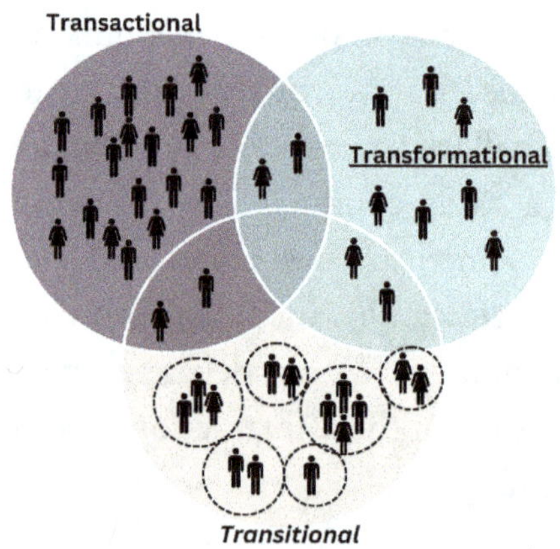

Classification or assignment will depend on various factors such as our methods of communication, the context for the interactions, and our personal development from the relationship. In assessing our relationships and our experiences within each category, we observe that while most relationships and their characteristics can be categorized distinctly, some may straddle multiple categories. We tend to allocate more time and energy to transformational relationships due to their potential for greater personal growth; however, every category holds its significance in our daily life. Moreover, it is not necessary for relationships to have a mutual perception (i.e., both parties see the relationship belonging to the same category). While symmetry might be beneficial, it's not a requisite akin to Newton's law.

How we've experienced our relationships distributed across the three categories is a majority of them will be in the Transactional and Transitional categories. Only a small minority (maybe ~20% of them, could be much less) will be in the Transformational category. For concepts on relationships in this book, we find that 80% of our time and effort will be applied to the 20% of our relationships in the Transformational category. This is due to the value that is found in these relationships.

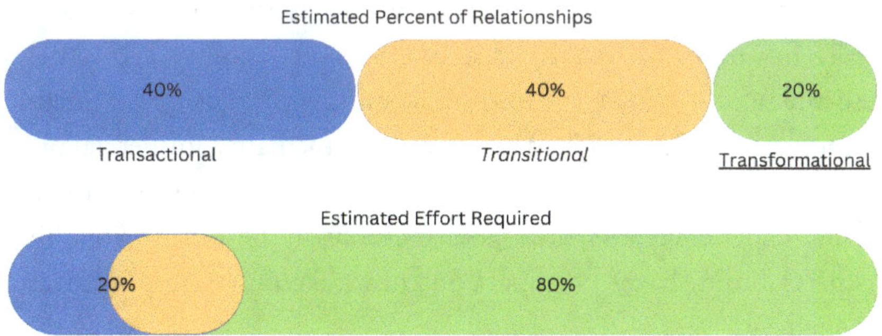

This initial math doesn't necessarily support the Pareto Principle, also known as the 80/20 rule, initially, but we do believe that in the limited amounts of Transformational relationships, we'll experience a high majority of our significant connections and bonds that will ultimately define our life story.

While common relationship labels such as romantic partners, parents, friends, neighbors, colleagues, and club associates are typically used, they all can be categorized into three primary classifications. This discussion will delve into the dynamics of these distinct types of relationships through the perspective of these three fundamental categories. Among those 610 relationships, a select few have the capacity to overlap and fulfill all three categories, although this is notably uncommon. Generally, once relationships solidify into a category, they remain there, though it's not unusual for them to shift between categories based on changes in personal circumstances or aspirations. Regarding the progression of Transitional-Transactional-Transformational relationships, one might wonder if it's feasible to bypass a stage of development. This largely depends on your personal aims and motivations. Given that only a minimal fraction of Transactional relationships evolve beyond the exchange itself, their primary role is often to nurture and capitalize on opportunities for new connections they may provide.

In the context of sales or business, interacting with potential clients can sometimes result in forming relationships with people you like personally, but may not lead to a deal or a hiring possibility. Nevertheless, these interactions can evolve into friendships with transitional qualities. Although such friendships may not yield immediate commercial or hiring gains, they provide mutual advantages through common interests and life experiences. As time goes by, even if the business or hiring prospects diminish, the personal bond can still retain its importance and be beneficial.

Ultimately, these relationship types demonstrate that understanding and skillfully managing Transactional, Transitional, and Transformational dynamics can make a meaningful difference in our personal development and the depth of our social connections.

Expectations for each chapter

While this isn't a textbook you won't find in school, we do follow the Apostle Paul and his letter to the Romans captured in Chapter 12, verse

2: "Do not conform any longer to the patterns of this world, or your friends, but be transformed by the renewing of your mind." We'll hope that you renew your mind with these concepts that we believe a lot of schooling ignores. They overlook the valuable insights of the different categories of relationships. In educational settings, group projects may exist, but they often prioritize subject matter expertise over team communication skills. Practical methods for improvement in relationship dynamics are often overlooked, even though they can significantly impact job performance and overall life satisfaction. I haven't experienced or heard of an example where an instructor's feedback focused on practical methods to improve in the relationship domain over more curriculum driven feedback.

However, the importance of relationships extends beyond just school projects or job reviews. The way we navigate our relationships can be a reflection of the value we place on our entire lives. When we categorize relationships and dedicate time and effort to nurture them, we work to achieve the desired, fruitful, outcomes at the highest level possible.

The following chapters will visit each category in detail, along with a small deep dive into the different phases that exist in transitional relationships. Each chapter's objective is to cover typical themes of the relationship category, the ways to identify them, how to embrace them, mature or walk away from them, and memorable tales relating to each category from our lives.

At the end, we will also highlight some specific applications of these categories as it pertains to parental relationships. This comes from two males' point of view so yes, it may seem limited. We see the concept so vital that even a limited view, a relationship with our children from a father's standpoint will provide valuable insight.

The task may overwhelm us when we think of all the relationships we are in, so to prevent the feeling we must focus on one relationship at a time. It allows us to understand:

That with every person we meet and in every discussion that takes place, we build each relationship into a beautifully, intertwined story full of <u>significance</u>.

The meaning of importance will differ from person to person, encompassing aspects such as economic achievement, celebrity, spiritual satisfaction, or self-improvement. This book is designed to offer you a framework and methodology to better steer through your current situation and shape your forthcoming experiences.

Please join us on this enlightening path as we dip into the realm of interpersonal connections, uncovering ways to comprehend and influence them to enrich our existence in manners that might have once seemed elusive.

"You are not a human being in search of a spiritual experience. You are a spiritual being immersed in a human experience." Pierre Telhard deChardin, a French idealist philosopher and Jesuit Catholic priest, stated in his writings in the 1950s

CHAPTER 2

Transactional Relationships

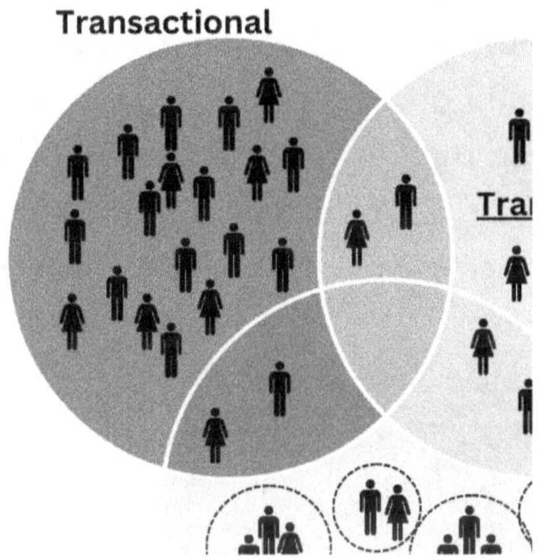

L et's start with a definition:

<u>Transaction</u>: *1) an exchange or transfer of goods, services, or funds 2) a communicative action or activity involving two parties or things that reciprocally affect or influence each other*

Participants in this type of relationship usually occupy the customer service aspect of an interaction, where <u>both</u> parties aim to benefit from a positive outcome. This could involve interactions with the cashier at your local grocery store, the last salesperson you made a purchase from, your friendly barista, or the last seller you encountered at a marketplace or craft show. Whether it's a doctor, a waitress, a front desk associate, a valet, or a flight attendant, these relationships revolve around how excellent service is delivered, all with the intention that you'll reciprocate with equal value, whether monetary or through referrals.

For a transactional relationship to work, there must be a clearly defined way to keep track of exchanges. There's little room to add extra value to the transaction, and carryover is rare. Essentially, it follows the principle of "I'll do for you what you do for me, no more, no less. If I sense you're not holding up your end, I'll seek a more 'equitable' exchange or find someone else who will."

Our estimations suggest that approximately 40% of the relationships we encounter throughout our lives can be classified in this manner. It is probable that additional relationships exist that don't immediately come to mind when thinking about "relationships." These aren't profound bonds and generally demand less commitment, aligning with the Pareto principle which asserts that one can obtain 80% of the outcomes from 20% of the effort.

A wealth of studies has been conducted on these types of connections. One particularly influential study was carried out by sociologist Mark Granovetter who looked into the dynamics of social networks and discovered the significant impact that casual acquaintances have in our lives. In his influential work "The Strength of Weak Ties," Granovetter presented the idea that such weak ties grant us access to fresh information, opportunities, and resources that our immediate circle of friends and family cannot provide.

His findings also pointed out the vital role weak ties play when it comes to seeking employment and advancing careers since they alert us to new job possibilities and can facilitate referrals. Additionally, he noted that weak ties serve an essential function in accessing resources, such as loans, guidance, or emotional support, and are especially beneficial for individuals actively job searching or undergoing major life transitions.

By examining the value of weak ties, Granovetter's research opposed the conventional belief that only strong relationships hold the highest significance in our social constructs. He suggested an alternative perspective, where weak ties deliver benefits distinct from those offered by our intimate networks. He further concluded that weak ties often arise from spontaneous meetings or unpredictable occurrences, underscoring the utility of engaging with new experiences and making new acquaintances.

In summary, Granovetter's insights into weak ties reveal that the breadth of our social networking profoundly influences our achievements and happiness, advocating that expanding our circle to encompass various weak ties yields substantial advantages personally and professionally. Should we effectively harness these associations with empathy, positivity, and authenticity, the opportunities they present can be astounding.

Transactional relationships might occur among colleagues from separate departments or business segments who are outside your immediate team circle. It's also possible to observe these relationships between managers and their direct reports, though it may represent the least beneficial type for such interactions. Furthermore, relationships with educators and family members can appear transactional in nature. However, these are often the initial instances where we might challenge their categorization as such. A deeper analysis of this will be presented in subsequent chapters.

My father frequently collaborated with inexperienced agents who assumed that their ability to make a sale was assured because they also intended to engage in a "reciprocal purchase" from the customer. They operated by the principle, "I will purchase only from those who are or could potentially become clients/customers." While this approach isn't inherently flawed, it does have inherent limitations. For instance, what happens if you're unable to fulfill their subsequent needs, or if the situation becomes one-sided with no reciprocation? Strategizing for the long-term use of this method is challenging.

In such sales contexts, same as the customer service situations mentioned before, we find ourselves in a dual role—acting as both purchaser and vendor. We understand the disappointment when the counterpart fails to fulfill their obligations.

Buyers & Sellers

Two key items to discern as we begin this chapter. First is to question if a relationship is transactional to begin with. If it is then we need to identify the buyer and seller in these relationships at the forefront. I.e. Do we want what they offer, or is it the other way around?

1. *Is there a shared common goal between the two parties?*
    1. *Transactional relationships generally lack a shared common goal.*
2. *Is there a way to measure the exchanges?*
    1. *Transactional relationships are quantifiable*
3. *Is the exchange equitable?*
    1. *Transaction relationships involve an equal or "quid pro quo" exchange.*

The final clarification, "Is the exchange equitable?" can be complex as the answer may never be entirely clear but to optimize the relationship we must know the balance. When we have equitable exchanges, the relationship is simple in nature and both buyer and seller can work on their side of the scale to grow naturally.

When the value isn't evenly balanced, it raises questions about whether it's a healthy form of this relationship (on its way towards a transitional or transformational category) or an unhealthy one that borders on a waste of time and resources.

When an unhealthy, unequal exchange is accepted, it plants the seeds of manipulation and unhealthy behaviors.

This isn't always the case, but this where internal conflicts arise between the heart and mind. In such situations, we rely on our intuition and seek counsel from other transformational relationships to better understand the dynamics. This might be evident in the smooth-talking salesperson who employs a short-sighted strategy with a focus on volume rather than quality. If you find yourself on the buy side of this transaction, it's best to address it directly and swiftly, and minimize any potential fallout. One should opt for the path of least resistance and steer clear of unequal transactional relationships.

On the rarest occasion, some healthy and yet unequal transactional relationships may become examples of a relationship that could develop into one of the other categories. Rare being the key word as even in my father's and I life we've only had maybe five or six relationships make the voyage. When they do exist, it's typically a result of exceptional effort and an embrace of the transactional relationship on both sides. This provides a natural attraction for both participants to see the value in further evaluation.

When a transactional relationship ends, it leads to the simplest form of termination as the participants can simply walk away. Additional time spent to justify the termination is not worth the investment as the reason is typically due to equal value not being returned. It's important to highlight the simplicity since the other two categories require processes to better identify healthy ways to cope with the termination.

"There is nothing innately good about inevitable failure!", David Gibson, Living Life Backward.

It's fairly common to encounter situations where the interaction is centered around "scorekeeping" and comparing accomplishments based on certain standards. In these cases, one might adopt a mindset of "comparison-driven growth and jealousy," emphasizing how we stack up against others instead of focusing on our own growth. This behavior is symptomatic of relationships that are stagnant at a transactional stage. By contrast, in transformational relationships, it is beneficial to be surrounded by people who encourage you to meet unwavering, transformative standards.

Embrace the Transaction

This portion examines seller-focused methods to deliver outstanding customer service with integrity, emphasizing equal buyer engagement. It's not about manipulation but applying tactics from icons like Dale Carnegie, Zig Ziglar, and Mike Weinberg. We recognize what makes a successful sale from our experiences, yet implementing these techniques can be difficult.

The key building blocks to optimize these interactions lie in offering empathetic, positive, and authentic energy.

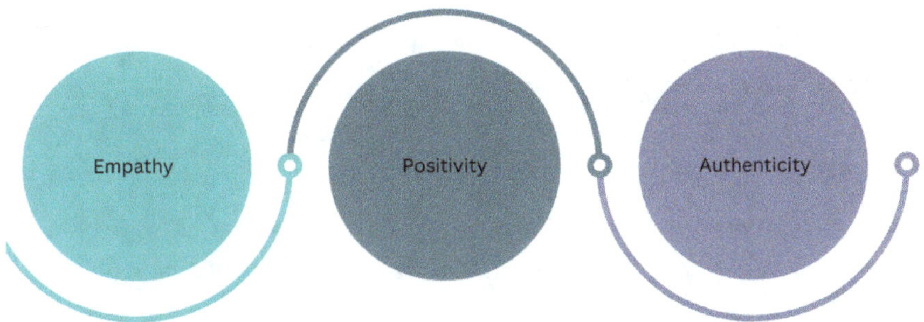

Empathetic

Initially we believed that being "enthusiastic" would yield the highest value in these relationships. Yet, upon deeper reflection, we recognized the potential drawback when the buyer isn't in a particularly "cheery" mood. There have been instances where I've arrived at a hotel to check in for a late-night, midweek stay, fatigued from a day of travel. In such situations, the last thing I desired was an overly energetic individual the bombarded me with questions about my day and an exhaustive spiel about hotel amenities, including intricate details about weekend pool hours. What I wanted then was empathy—to have them understand that I simply needed my room key, directions to my room, and perhaps a complimentary bottle of water. On the other hand, if I'm checking in for a week-long family vacation at a resort, high energy and detailed information about pool hours are entirely welcome. Empathy is what buyers often seek; they hope the seller can resonate with their energy naturally.

While these interactions might not be a seller's top priority, we must recognize their initial enthusiasm. As we exhibit empathy, we can now focus on the other two traits: positivity and authenticity.

Positive

We'll keep this section brief because it's straightforward. Although it's easier to discuss and engage with topics from a negative standpoint, a negative outlook will taint Transactional relationships.

"Optimism is the faith that leads to achievement. Nothing can be done without hope and confidence." - Helen Keller

"Positive thinking is more than just a tagline. It changes the way we behave. And I firmly believe that when I am positive, it not only makes me better, but it also makes those around me better." - Harvey Mackay

For productive Transactional relationships on both sides, the seller typically leads with the positive mindset. Positive discourse leads to fruitful outcomes and revitalizes emotional and mental energy instead of one that causes a negative drain.

Authentic

We're striving for an experience that's dynamic and genuine. My family knows all too well that when I'm talking to customer service and I get subpar replies like "I don't make the policy" or hear dispassionate tone in phrases like "yes, this is an unfortunate situation," it really gets under my skin. Like many people, often in these situations it's not about getting something in return or expecting a problem to be fixed on the spot, but it's about sensing if the person on the other end of the line truly understands our point of view, even if we may be mistaken.

Authenticity drives natural interactions that foster trust and results in a stronger bond between the parties involved.

A familiar situation where these traits coalesce is in interviews. When I'm in the interviewer's role, I have the ability to set the conversational tone. In consulting, new engagements typically involve numerous interviews. This isn't a job interview (we usually have some form of commitment secured), but rather a chance to engage with everyone from C-suite executives to analysts, managers to field technicians. The objective is to gain insights through tactical and tailored questions, that in turn makes our job more manageable. We want interviewees to provide answers that point us in the right direction, help us understand where to focus, and warn us about potential pitfalls.

Regardless of their title or position on the organizational chart, we encounter various personalities and attitudes. There are those who resist change relentlessly, the irrationally furious ones who claim to have already conveyed the same information to leadership, and the confident "know-it-alls." However, our largest challenge is with the "disengaged."

The disengaged often offer cleaver and successful solutions, but any engagement with them requires substantial effort. They may have been let down in the past and now merely go through the motions each day, or they might have felt unheard for so long that they've given up on any sort of back-and-forth communication. They typically see-through corporate jargon and grasp the true situation. Fancy dinners or free lunches won't entice them to open up.

What works is quality time and trust, and we're fortunate if we have 30 to 60 minutes to achieve that. It's important to not start on the wrong foot with these individuals like many colleagues and myself have fallen into before. We might unintentionally echo corporate jargon we believe will impress them, only to see them retreat into a shell of indifference. At times, we might mirror their disengagement (often due to the monotony of four or five identical interviews in a day), then rush to conclude the conversation and end up with the same result.

The simplest solution in such cases is sometimes to avoid the initiative altogether in discussions. I might ask, "What motivates you to come to work in the morning?" or "Who at the office provides a dose of humor?" Keep in mind that we attempt to uncover why the client has experienced poor margins or throughput issues. These questions typically catch the disengaged off guard. The aim is to get them to talk about anything. Delve into tangents and tease out the details. They have a plan in mind, one they've rehearsed and refined over months or years, and our task is to coax it out. Once we understand the context behind their disengagement (like the promotion they were denied two years ago or their perception of a disconnect with leadership), we acknowledge it.

We may not be able to address it in the scope of our engagement, but ***we must be empathetic to their thoughts and authentically address the situation to keep the remainder of the conversation positive.*** This signifies that we're in this together and intend to move forward in unison.

Sometimes, interviewees lack any ulterior motives and are simply disengaged from the organization or the process. This attitude often becomes a topic that we need to uncover and discuss with leadership because it may be the employee's authentic self... which is a little scary. While our engagement's focus isn't on these interviewees, they serve as conduits to navigate the numerous transactional relationships we'll encounter to achieve overall success.

Whether we're buyers or sellers, these transactional relationships offer ample opportunities to refine how we listen. We can experiment with various strategies to identify what works best and translate what we hear into thoughts that train our minds with useful effective memory techniques.

We gather insights when we listen and dedicate more time to understand the context of the other participant rather than formulate any potential rebuttals or stories from our own experiences. Although it's natural for humans to want to challenge others' statements or respond with a more impressive story, it's not worth the energy. That energy can better shape your own thoughts and provide additional context for the next interaction with another relationship.

Why invest all this effort in this category of relationship? It's about the process, the preparation, and capability to hone our cognitive abilities and instincts for <u>when they matter most</u> in the subsequent two relationship categories.

Transactional Tales

As we consolidate all these applications and stories into more personal stories we can't stress how numerous and diverse they are, but as we reflected with Granovetter's research, just how valuable they can be. Now here are some tales may be light in nature, but others will showcase just how valuable.

Doctors

One of the most relatable examples is the transactional relationship we all share with a doctor. Even at 32, the idea of visiting the doctor still makes me apprehensive. Over time, I've realized that my fear is more about what the doctor might convey rather than the setting itself. Their demeanor heavily influences the entire interaction. Just picture yourself in that examination room, awaiting the doctor's diagnosis. Wouldn't you prefer the doctor to exhibit these three traits—empathy, positivity, and authenticity—as they walk in? If the doctor embodied the best aspects of these qualities, I believe I could handle whatever news they might have to deliver.

Valet

While I worked as a valet in college, I would typically work the weekends and was the face of the hotel for many of the guests that make their weekend get-aways up to the beautiful tip of Lake Superior (in the summer/fall that is). It was always fun to meet the new guests on Friday night, understand if it was for a wedding, for family, yearly trips, tourism, etc. and through their time there, it was great to interact with them. I was a pretty good valet, but I made my fair share of mistakes in my shifts. Whether I messed up a guest's last name, recommended restaurants not even close to what they had expected, didn't have their car out front when they wanted it, or not out front to help with bags when they arrived, it wasn't anything major, but still I wanted to provide the best service (yes in hopes of good tips, but I was a college kid). My biggest fear was that my mistakes would always "follow" the same guests all weekend, and sure enough that did happen every so often.

When it came time for the guest to check out, in those instances, I found a way to apologize for the mistakes and hope they had another weekend trip planned where I could rectify it. To my surprise, the guests were typically naïve to the mistakes. The guests would only comment on some of the interactions where these key Transactional characteristics took place (I didn't know they were key back then) and how they enjoyed the service I provided. I first thought they were just being "Minnesota nice", but as those answers started to become more common.

I then I realized if I always came with "energy" that would make more of an impression to the guests rather than if a car was 2-3 minutes late.

Was it more than just energy? I think so in retrospect, but the job became a lot simpler when I just had to focus on one thing and apply that to the next activity rather than to try and manage the 20 other concurrent activities.

These interactions also paid off in the end when they provided me my first full-time career opportunity. I owe my marriage, current occupation, and much of my Transformational friends to a guest and the initial Transactional relationship but we'll get more into that later.

Transactional Tales (cont.)

Carpenter Turned Salesman

James Johnson>> *The transactions Josiah has discussed were ingrained in me as a child. My father was a brilliant salesman, encased in the body of a carpet-layer, who built a very successful carpet and flooring installation service after he was forced to close his furniture store. He developed a reputation in the community that he kept his word, honored his commitments and delivered an excellent product. He believed in "value added" to every interaction with his customers and contracts, and even wore a "tied" bowtie on the job because he saw himself as a "professional" just like the Banker, or Doctor, or Lawyer. When I graduated from college with a degree in Philosophy, there was little demand for philosophers since the end of the Vietnam debacle, so I went to work with my father.*

After college I worked with my father for two years until one wintery February day when a gentleman by the name of Bob Sparboe bought me a cup of coffee at the Colonial Café in Litchfield and recruited me to come work for him and his company. I was to be his egg salesman and develop their retail egg business. I told him I was flattered and honored by his offer, but I knew flooring, not agriculture or eggs. Bob persisted and told me he was recruiting me, not for my product knowledge which he would teach me, but for my people skills and my ability to develop and grow relationships which he had observed. I worked with Bob for over two years and received a "hands on" business education better than any business school could offer and an apprenticeship under Robert Sparboe. I was paid on commission only and was content until Bob asked me to switch from commission to salary. My father's wisdom was so ingrained in me that I thought a salary penalized great salespeople and promoted mediocrity, so I resigned in July of 1977 and went to work with my father.

That time spent with my father allowed me to build relations with the businesses we served and the contractors who used our services. My father was a master in sliding the Transactional/Transitional relationships with clients/customers and building our key clients into transformational rela-tionships. I worked with my father for another five years until I was physi-cally forced to make a new career decision.

An extremely critical conversation ensued with my father at a restau-rant over lunch when I told him I was going to leave to go to work for the New York Life Insurance Company. He smiled at me and told me "It was time to do that which gave me joy "and that he worked every day, not for the money but because he enjoyed the people we met and worked with. He was energized by the relationships! Even though my father has been gone now for over 30 years I still hear his words of wisdom!

After I made the switch to insurance I decided to stay in my hometown and build a business where I knew the community and the people in the community. One of my new prospects and soon to be clients was a long-term customer of my father. He approached me one morning at the local restaurant and asked me if my dad and I would be able to do some work for him at one of his properties. When I told him that I'm sure my dad would be able to help him, and I would pass on the message he asked me what I was doing and why I left my father's business. When I told him that I could no longer physically work with my father so I had entered the insurance business he asked for my card and wanted to set up a time to dis-cuss how my services would be able to help him and his business. I followed through on the transactional relationship and in turn developed the rela-tionship, which my father had initiated 10 years earlier, and transformed my father's client into my client and experienced how the process my father had started bore fruit.

Transactional Tales (cont.)

S**peak Up in Class**

I've had the opportunity to speak in a couple of different college classrooms relative to manufacturing and operations management. Try as I might to entertain on the topic, learning curve design or stocking strategies just don't engage a classroom of pupils. I give props to the professors that can do it day in and day out, and thankful they haven't necessarily asked me for my teaching prowess on the matter. They want me to give the students a glimpse of what's out there, and what it takes to be successful as they know bookwork will only get their students so far. It was in one of my last classes where that a student raised their hand with a question on whether my firm was hiring. I asked him in front of his peers if he was good. He responded with confidence that he thought so. I let the entire class know that we don't take many gambles on new hires, but if you had good experience, we would consider anyone interested.

To his credit, the student who asked the question did reach out, and we had an initial interview. His experience was enough to the partners and his personality that got him in the door continued to impress. From a question in class, to a job offer within about 6 weeks.

Right place, right time and understanding Transactional relationship dynamics is definitely a theme to much of life's opportunities, but it still requires action to realize it.

He has shown and continues to execute at equal levels of seasoned colleagues due to his internal drive and smarts.

Transitional Relationships

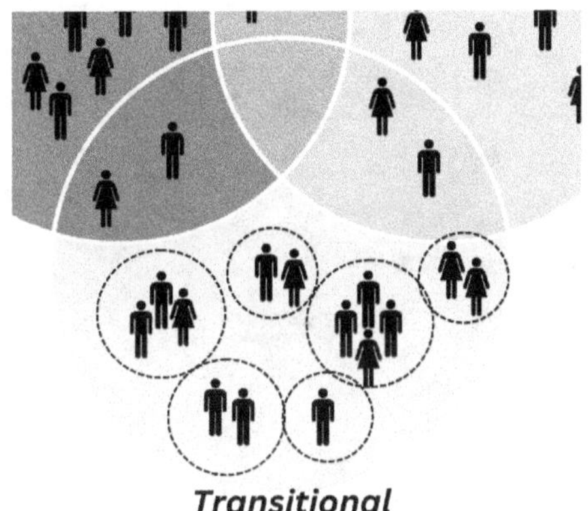

We've already discussed the most basic category of relationships, but it's not the first that we'll encounter. What about the relationships that are closest to us that we didn't choose in the first place. Those that we may have just been presented with potentially from birth. This category may make up most of the remaining relationships with about 40% of all the relationships we'll experience in life. They require more effort than quick, transactional connections, yet less effort than the profound transformational relationships, in terms of maintenance and growth. Transitional relationships are defined by two main factors: <u>environment</u> and <u>time</u>. The environment is crucial because it limits our choices for relationships in this category. These environments include places like schools, religious groups, sports teams, and especially the careers we desire. Time is also significant since the duration of these relationships depends on the situation. Typically, they last anywhere from 6 months to 6 years. Just as we can't control the environment, we also have limited control over how long these relationships endure.

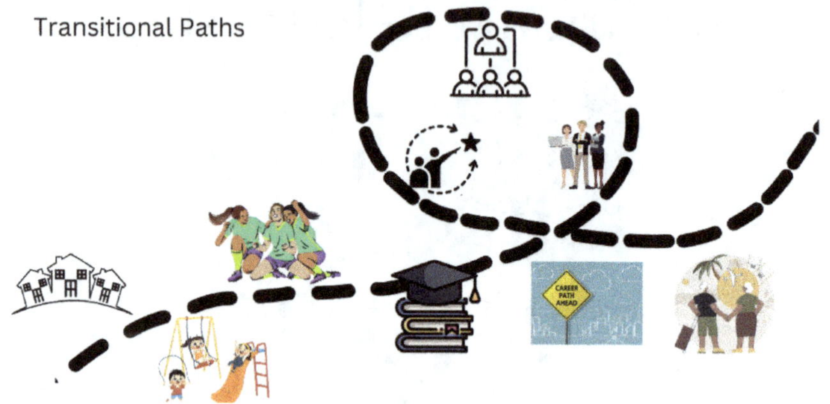

To try and think about those environments, we may need to think about our progression in life where we'll pass through three major phases of transitional relationships. We'll refer to the first phase as "the impressionable years." This phase spans from the earliest attempts at communication to our early 20s. The next is naturally the "career years" which extends for the next 30 to 40 years, until the final "2nd Stage" relationship phase.

During the <u>impressionable years</u> of transitional relationships, our selection of relationships will be the most limited even though they have a significant impact on our lives. You'll recognize these relationships are based upon the neighborhoods where you grew up, initial school classrooms and through sports teams. They are discovered in the religious or hobby groups you joined, or better the ones a parent or guardian signed you up for as a child. They may only act as the steppingstones to the next level. In the impressionable years, immaturity was common, as long-term perspective was distorted by our age and surroundings. In this life phase, we were either stubborn or incapable to make a deeper commitment to have the relationships move forward. Generally, we either enjoyed or endured these relationships due to a lack of maturity, perspective, and commitment. Unfortunately, some relationships never evolve past this stage and remain long after their initial temporary nature

It's not necessarily a problem to remain at this level; however, just as a ship is built for the open seas, we were meant for more than to just stay in the harbor.

The transitional relationships in our early careers exhibit similar dynamics to the prior phase. They are the relationships we encounter as we begin to establish our own residences in new cities or just on the other side of town. These relationships also include the professional teams we join at work or in associations with like-minded individuals. The piece that ties these relationships together are the external goals. External goals are what the businesses or groups are focused on (selling goods, making goods, the topic of discussion) rather than the internal goals such as personal growth or promotion. It's often in our professional life where we interview for the job description and not for the future co-workers. We soon realize these relationships, where we didn't select them, have significant impact on our job, which we did select, in both performance and satisfaction. This is the key attribute that captures the "limited selection" aspect, which applies to both job opportunities and the individuals who become our colleagues.

The final phase, the 2nd Stage, is where time becomes the primary factor for participants in the relationship. Typically, the participants are in a retirement age group, and the focus shifts more towards belonging, enjoyment and satisfaction rather than personal or professional growth.

Environmental Controls

Similar to transactional relationships, there are a few questions we can ask to determine whether we're in an environment and time-controlled relationship:

1. *Are all participants in this group working for the same external goals*
    1. *Transitional relationships have the same or similar external goals.*
2. *Can issues be escalated to a superior for resolution?*
    1. *Transitional relationships exist in an environment where the participants can be escalated to a superior.*
3. *Is the relationship forced by a physical location?*
    1. *Transitional relations are generated and forced by the physical location(s)*

If the answer is "yes" to any of them, then the relationship is transitional. As we've teased before, each identified phase has their own nuances to these answers, but the basis remains unchanged

One might argue that managers and directors who are responsible for hiring have a say in who joins the team which would suggest that these relationships might not be transitional. However, as we've previously mentioned, leaders should select and hire individuals with whom they can build transformational relationships. Hiring individuals merely for transactional or transitional purposes is shortsighted, expensive, and unlikely to yield the potentially life-changing results.

Throughout the subsequent chapters regarding the work-specific transitional relationships, we'll approach the topic from a same work group, colleague-to-colleague perspective and not based upon superior/subordinate view.

Transient Selection

Transitional relationships are natural candidates evolve into transformational ones. While that's a goal for most meaningful relationships, we may only find a few that we truly desire to elevate to that level. To help with the search, we further categorize the types of transitional relationships as *nurturing*, *escalating* and *tolerating*.

When aiming for long-term benefits, it's important to invest time and effort into nurturing the relationship. For short-term benefits, decide if the relationship can be managed with minimal effort and aligns with your goals. If not, escalation might be necessary to ensure we don't waste any time and likely our emotional and mental health on aspects outside of our control. Alternatively, the relationship might evolve to a point where the participant's stance is unmovable, in which case toleration becomes the logical choice. Categorizing relationships this way can improve your quality of life and help avoid constant challenges.

Too much time and resources are often wasted in when we try to revive a relationship that is unlikely to succeed. The next three chapters will provide how we can apply these labels across the transitional phases.

Stagnant Vs. Transitional Relationships

The natural progression and inflection point of transitional relationships in this category often lead to a straightforward ending.

The environment changes...

Co-workers move on to new roles, courses come to an end, sports seasons conclude, or new small groups are formed. While the transitional nature might suggest ending such relationships, making that decision is much more challenging in our everyday lives. We are people with feelings at the end of the day. When evaluating a "stagnant" relationship, one where the environment and time have run out, the evaluation centers around whether the external goals that were present in the environment have translated into similar internal, more personal goals. If not, the best practice is to communicate your personal goals, if asked, and work towards mutually beneficially concluding the relationship.

If goals have <u>transcended</u>, the next evaluation becomes whether you have the time and energy to foster the relationship's development. The effort to maintain the natural rhythm for the growth becomes a challenge to that development. If you can't commit sufficient time and energy, ending the relationship becomes a logical step.

A cause for concern arises when the environment no longer exists, goals are misaligned, yet the relationship continues with no potential for growth.

From our own experiences, tolerating a misaligned transitional relationship for too long can cause *more* pain and harm. People may spend years chasing unclear goals and end up in places they didn't expect or intend. Wanting something better is good, but it's important not to overestimate your abilities. Maybe you think you don't have the skills, talent, or education to move forward on your own, so you rely on someone else for help. This isn't necessarily a problem if you're honest about your intentions, but it's important to use your charm and appeal to improve your situation.

We need to have a perspective that will allow us to fail our failures fast.

It's okay to rely on someone's support, but when you stop, the relationship might end, leaving you wondering what's next. This often happens because you can't see the bigger picture or lack confidence, hoping the relationship will help you grow or find new opportunities. You might also get tired of relationships that go nowhere. **Dead-end**

jobs and stagnant relationships tend to go hand in hand. To escape, you might jump into a new relationship for fresh opportunities. So, because of a lack of vision, confidence, and perseverance, you look for a new and better place through a new opportunity, person, or challenge. Is this wrong? Not if you're honest with everyone involved, including yourself. Did you get what you wanted and reach your goal? Be truthful! If a relationship becomes transformational, it might cause lasting harm to you or the other person. It's important to spend time nurturing a potential relationship. This shows why it's crucial to carefully choose and manage transitional relationships to make the most of them.

Transitional Embrace

While transitional relationships can be volatile, they can offer lasting benefits. Much of the embrace will be catered to the phase you are in. Based on our experiences, we've identified a couple of techniques that accelerate the development of these relationships and enhance productive outcomes for both parties across all phases. One of these techniques involves adopting a "cheerleader mentality" when approaching interactions and discussions within this relationship category.

This cheerleader mentality entails that we offer unwavering positive support, regardless of the circumstances. It means being someone who encourages and energizes others. Staying in line with this mindset, it's crucial to focus on team accomplishments and each individual's contributions.

A cheerleading approach leaves no room for ego or politics. This allows you to become a dependable and steady voice that others can rely on.

Early in my career, I crossed paths with a versatile team member, let's call him Jimmy. Jimmy joined my network of transitional relationships when we were assigned to manage a section of the final assembly line together—he oversaw the people, and I managed the process. Right from the start, Jimmy approached every morning meeting, coffee chat, or intense strategy session with the same positive attitude. He connected well with the workforce, and his supportive attitude was evident in his interactions.

It's worth noting that having a cheerleader mindset requires a certain degree of inherent personality traits. Faking it can come off as.... awkward. Jimmy's approach was genuine, rooted deep within him. For those of us where it might not come as naturally, the key is to keep the support and tone consistent and "expected." When people know you're a cheerleader in their corner, they're more likely to communicate openly, discuss challenging topics, and express raw emotions. This naturally draws out how we will nurture, escalate, or tolerate these individuals. This contributes to more meaningful discussions and actions both in the workplace and in our personal lives, compared to a situation where uncertainty surrounds the availability of support.

The second technique might seem contradictory to the first, but we see them as complementary. This technique involves not being a "yes man or yes woman," but instead, allows us to approach topics objectively and challenge them with alternative perspectives or seek additional ideas.

To put it differently; **bring the cheer, but callout the bullshit.**

By presenting alternatives or encouraging other ideas, we maintain a level of the cheerleading approach. When people come to us with problems or suggestions, they know what to expect. We might not always provide the "right" answer or feel that we add immediate value, but the trust that develops is what leads to long-term success, rather than seeking a quick, short-lived revelation. As we delve into examples, you'll notice these two techniques at play.

Transitional Illustrations

Before jumping into more personal stories of relationships in this category, we think it's advantageous to highlight more popular stories seen in media that characterize transitional relationships, but more importantly showcase when and how they were utilized, but also where there was stagnation that we may all emphasize with.

Pat McAfee Show

Before September 2022, the name Pat McAfee might not have been widely recognized by many, aside from being a retired athlete appearing on a YouTube show while discussing "Covid Toe." However, following September 2022, McAfee's presence in the news increased significantly as he embarked on a rapid journey to revolutionize the sports experience, aiming for a more authentic and immersive approach. By fall of 2023, he had joined ESPN as a staple program, hosting a two-hour show on weekdays. While this ascent might seem like a whirlwind, it's not a new concept for McAfee; he and his friends-turned-co-workers have been navigating this path since retiring from football in February 2017. McAfee's utilization in this book is primarily due to his keen understanding and application of "Transitional" relationships, along with his involvement in the other categories.

McAfee's introduction to media began with sold-out comedy shows, interviews, and content creation for Barstool Sports. He engaged in commentary and performances in major stadiums around wrestling rings, culminating in the creation of "The Pat McAfee Show." Through these ventures, McAfee and his team (referred to as "PMS" collectively) gained insights valuable to modern media platforms such as Twitter, YouTube, and satellite radio. PMS ventured into these new environments without knowing their eventual destination or timeline but remained committed to their brand of sports media and reporting.

Starting with a Barstool partnership, PMS began streaming on Sirius XM. As the team later revealed during non-Sirius stream times and after-hours sessions, broadcast live on YouTube, their relationship with Sirius evolved from the nurturing phase to a state of escalating dissatisfaction. The inequity in transactions prompted PMS to pursue escalation. While viewers could sense the strain, PMS recognized that this transitional relationship was a stepping stone to the next one, requiring another bet on themselves. They continued to tolerate the Sirius deal while also securing a substantial agreement with FanDuel, a sports betting turned television platform. While larger media and television companies acknowledged PMS's success, they didn't fully grasp the magnitude of what PMS had achieved: a revolutionary change in the sports landscape.

Understanding the significance of "PMS" over "McAfee" is pivotal at this juncture. The show's essence doesn't solely reside in McAfee; it's the collective effort of the team around him. Many co-hosts and talents on the primary program are McAfee's childhood friends who have grown with the grassroots show, eventually becoming hosts on their own platforms. This team also includes retired NFL general managers and former hockey professionals. McAfee's approach to business, distinct from his attitude towards "suits" in larger media companies, centers on trust and exposure for his team. This has been the catalyst for top-tier television content. He has nurtured extended transitional and even transformational relationships within his team, showcasing them both on and off-screen. This sets him apart, as other media teams often struggle to achieve the same level of unity.

Even as PMS transitions from its FanDuel partnership to a potentially controversial one with Disney/ESPN, many loyal listeners who have been tuning in since 2018 anticipate what the future holds for members like Ty Schmit, Connor Campbell (Boston Connor), Anthony DiGuilio (Tone Digz), Kyle Cathcart (Bubba Gumpino), Evan

Foxy, Frank (Nick) Maraldo, and Zito Perez, along with others who started in a box truck and those who continue to join the team.

McAfee's ability to swiftly discern different relationships, whether with the business itself or the individuals within it, and drive growth towards a shared goal, is a quality all leaders should aspire to possess. While we find ourselves in the midst of McAfee's and the PMS team's journey, the foundations of their business and relationships are clearly visible. Another narrative that is currently evolving is that of Michael Vick. While Vick is now a recognizable figure on television, his story also includes documentaries and books about his prominence in the early 2000s.

Transitional Illustrations

Michael Vick

Michael Vick was one of my favorite athletes growing up, along with a lot of other kids (and adults) that had watched him play football at Virginia Tech and then in the NFL with the Atlanta Falcons. In the 2001 draft he became the first African American Quarterback (QB) ever selected #1 overall, and after his fourth season he signed a nine-year $130M extension with a $37M signing bonus. 2 years later he became the first QB to rush over 1,000 yards in a single season. By the end of 2006, his estimated annual income between his NFL Salary and endorsements was at $25.4M. He was on a trajectory that few ever dream of, but quickly crashed a few months later when he pled guilty to federal charges associated with a dog fighting investigation. Vick was sentenced to 23 months in prison.

"As I started to turn the corner, as I started to see life different, I got a young daughter at the time, I got a son that's like 4, as I'm starting to make change, it's just a little too late..." Michael Vick, Club Shay Shay Podcast

At the time this was quite a whirlwind of emotions following the athlete I idolized have this kind of past. Today, Vick has rebounded his career and I enjoy seeing him again on Sundays as an analyst with Fox Sports and venturing into new docu-series. I was always interested in his life because he had to live through the highs of his promising career and through guilt and shame of his actions in a very public light and it left me wondering "how". How did he come to get into this position. It didn't happen overnight. It wasn't an accident. Vick has recently gone on a podcast with Shannon Sharpe named "Club Shay Shay" where Sharpe asked him a lot of questions related to his time leading up to the federal charges. Below is an excerpt from the podcast:

Vick is adamant in the interview that it was not his friends, but his own decisions to follow through with his actions that got him in trouble. In respect to the relationships highlighted in this book, these Transitional relationship between Vick and his friends were comfortable, but they both sides were not striving towards to same goals. Vick goes on:

I would have known better. If I would have known better, I would have done better I promise you...

Had he have known better. I think we all sympathize with that thought in our own lives. According to the interview, Vick's friends were trying to tell him, but those relationships hadn't transcended to a transformational relationships. Vick could have been better off with a new Transitional relationship...one with others in the league who had been there, had seen a bit of the success, and been able to say to him 'I see where this journey may take you'.

'SS: Is there any friends that you could have had? If you could have surrounded yourself with some different people, do you think the situation would have been different. What could Michael Vick have done differently to have a different outcome?

MV: Listen to my Mom... when she found out what was going on, she was like you need to stop doing what you doing... I got 13M in the bank, I got money in there. I'm looking at her like 'Mom I'm alright. I got it, everything under control...I'm lying to her... My Mom looked me in the eyes one day and she was like "You're not happy"...I got all this, I got everything.

SS: Why did she think you weren't happy?

MV: A lot of guilt to what I was doing. Had a lot of other situations going on with Kids, with family, my son, going through it with his mom, so I just wasn't in a good place in 2006-2007, I was really searching for happiness when I had everything that I thought I wanted. Everything I worked hard for in life. This was before anything even popped off...There were a lot of people coming to me to get me on the right track.

SS: ...You have everything you had hoped for, but you didn't have peace.

MV: I didn't have peace.

You can see where Shannon Sharpe was going with his questions. In Vick's responses, he comes back to a very natural response of his mother. Family wisdom can typically always be available but seldom followed as it is seemingly entangled with egos, history, and sense of family one-sidedness. That's when our friends, our transitional and transformational relationships really come into play.

Dave Ramsey has a quote "Surround yourself with people who add the fuel of advice and encouragement to your fire." Vick had the fuel, but where was his fire going.

MV: (Referring to 2007-2008 year) And they were teaching me out to play the QB position, for protections. We were starting all over in a new system. Hue's (Jackson) like 'man, you're going to be the league MVP this year' and I really felt that way cause my focus was different. A lot of my boys moved out the house, we was living together. My wife moved in, my daughter. So, I was turning the corner. It was just too late. Everything was starting to take a turn for the worse. That year we would have gone deep in the playoffs, I definitely would have been on a hall of fame path for sure....

SS: You mentioned that you had your boys in the home, before you had moved your wife in with your daughter. What did they bring, what were they telling you.... What are they adding to Michael Vick's football life?

MV: They supported me a lot. When I started to lose.....It was like motivational speeches, 'you need to stop doing this, you need to stop'....

SS: Mike, what good is it to have friends if you ain't listening?

MV: That's what I'm saying man, my life is one big misconception. People think it was my boys were my downfall. Nah, they were some of my biggest supporters. They were just in a position where they go too hard on me 'Don't do this, don't do that'....I hated that they felt that they were in that situation.... I never looked at it that way. I might have had an attitude of been a little upset, but I'm not going to kick my man to the curb just for telling me to stop drinking the yak.

"What good is it to have <u>relationships</u> if you aren't listening?" is the million-dollar question. Relationships will shape our lives one way or another. Though Vick's relationships didn't bring him down the road he was heading, Vick didn't allow himself to have anyone else to divert or correct him.

Transitional Relationships–Impressionable Years

Transitional Paths

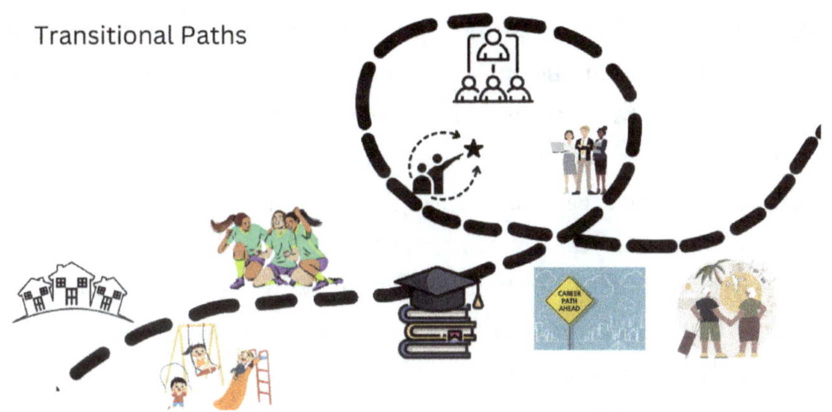

Take a moment to reflect on your friends from preschool, the local park and summer camps. How many of these connections have endured and you would invite them over for dinner this week? How many high school reunions have you attended, and among those, how many of your former friends appear unchanged after 10, 25, or 50 years? Many transitional relationships persisted due to consistent interaction and an openness to each participant's growth, benefiting from cherished memories created through activities like after-school events, birthday parties, and collaborative efforts on school activities. However, once high school ended or neighborhoods changed, these relationships often lacked a foundation to sustain them, leading them to naturally fade away. Nothing negative occurred; life simply moved forward.

Now consider reunions, whether high school or college. How many of those past relationships were joyful to rekindle? If you enjoyed the reunion, would you actively arrange another meeting, understanding that the conversation might be limited unless you both found new common ground to build a fresh connection?

Limited Control Application

I'll assume most readers are reflecting on this era rather than experiencing it presently. The significance of transitional relationships during our formative years lies in the fact that they often contributed to our personal transformations, but the relationships may not have been a transformational one. These relationships helped shape our identities and influenced our dreams and thought patterns for the good and the bad that ultimately affect the way we navigate life today.

For those who've found themselves repeatedly stated "how did I end up here", they may have overlooked past relationships that may have overstayed their welcome. It's an intricate process to recognize and categorize these relationships as they occur during our adolescent years.

If we find ourselves still in them, the reactive approach is to move forward, without any further dedicated time, energy, and effort to connections that we can now accurately categorize and address. It's important to understand that this is only when we can have clarity that the current relationship has "expired" and the environment no longer exists.

I frequently discuss this concept with my girls, currently in fourth and sixth grade. Their closest friends are those they met during preschool and kindergarten. Much of their happiness, hurt, and enjoyment stem from these connections, even though they had a pool of 20 potential options. Why is it challenging to bond with others within that group? Why invest so much in a relationship that causes pain? Wrestling with these inherent human experiences sparks intriguing contemplation. Looking back at my elementary school friends, many of whom I haven't seen since the last day of high school, I'm reminded of similar patterns in middle school and high school. However, during my junior year of high school, I began to distinguish the "transitional" phases within relationships. Friends I had from birth, where the bond on fun memories where the only item keeping us together as our external goals had changed. This led to a fruitful shift in my friend circles. Just one year later, during my senior year new relationships developed and evolved into some of my closest, transformational relationships.

This leads us to an important juncture in this phase. As we discussed, a challenge of a transitional relationships is that some will develop without your active participation or even awareness of the transitional nature. My father's junior year of High School he participated in the Spring theatrical production and had "flirted" with one of the actresses and spent time with her at practice and occasionally during the school day. He hadn't realized that she read more into the relationship than he was. When Spring Prom approached, he asked if she would like to go with him to the dinner and dance and she said yes.

Well, what confused my father about this "date"was that he later discovered that she had hoped a Senior "jock" would ask her, but that jock had asked someone else, so my dad was the runner-up winner. She danced most of the evening with this Jock and my father learned a valuable lesson; define the potential relationship before you rent a tux! Lesson learned, no regrets, but now he knows the warning indicator lights of a transitional relationship.

Established timelines and expectations simplify the dynamics in Transitional relationships. While it may seem outdated, my grandmother advised my father not to become intimate with anyone he didn't see as a potential spouse. Ending a primarily physical relationship can be challenging. However, this perspective remains relevant and underscores the value of setting relationship boundaries. After 45 years, my father's *unmatched* transformational relationship with my mom, Peggy, is not even on the same level of the *mismatched* Transitional relationship he walked away from.

For many of us, college, vocational school, or the military expanded our world view for the first time. My father's most impactful transitional relationships were cultivated at St. Paul Bible College, now known as Crown College, where two professors significantly influenced his personal growth. Dr. John Gates, head of the philosophy department, guided him through the world of ancient and medieval philosophy, fostered an understanding of human potential and the unnecessary limitations we impose on ourselves. He learned so much from Dr. Gates about the potential God has placed within man and the limitations we have needlessly placed on ourselves. In his time with Dr. Gates, my father developed the realization that he had the ability to choose and build new relationships not tied to his past or history. That these new relationships were not constrained by neighborhood or graduation, location or time.

Another Professor, Professor Larson who taught English and creative writing, encouraged my father to write without restraint and embrace unique perspectives. Professor Larson transported him to a greater understanding of my God given creativity and the responsibility that I have as a steward of that God-given talent. Through these relationships, my father learned that he could build connections untethered from past boundaries, locations, or time.

When his class studied Socrates, my father learned a principle that he remembers every day; that "the unexamined life is not worth living" which Plato reported that Socrates uttered at his trial for impiety and corrupting youth. He modified this truth when he studied relationships, that the unexamined relationship is not worth the maintenance!

Multiple factors and experiences during these impressionable years mold us, but it's who is involved with us that ultimately refines us. Right or wrong, the environment you found yourself in became the persona that you live with. Many of us may be embarrassed of this now but may serve as our drive to evolve. Evolve both internally and in the relationships, we are in as they act as our catalyst for growth and future potential transformation. We truly have limited control in these relationships, but there still is some control.

CHAPTER 5

Transitional Relationships– Career Years

Transitional Paths

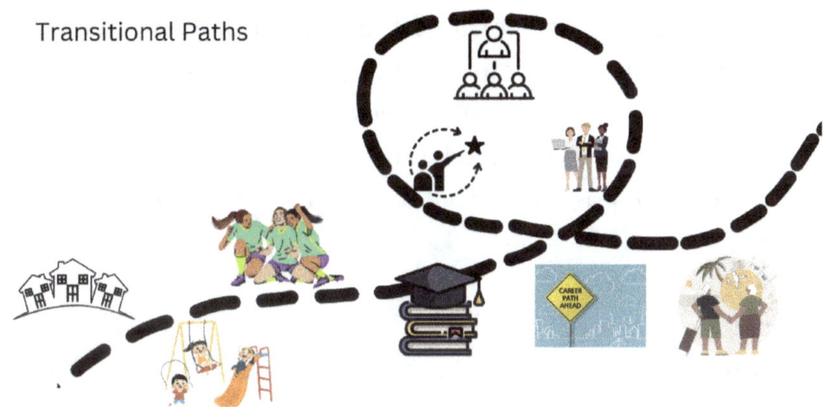

During the next transitional phase of our lives, we encounter peers within the professional realm as we embark on careers. We end up spending A LOT of time with these individuals. Individuals that play into our weekly experiences and hope to find fulfillment in every day activities. The stakes are high, and the nature of the relationships we encounter vary based on our chosen field and personal aspirations for growth. Whether we move across the country or remain close to our hometown, new transitional relationships will emerge.

A significant characteristic of these transitional relationships is that while we have chosen the professional environment, <u>we haven't necessarily selected the individuals within it</u>.

Often, we prioritize career, societal, or religious affiliations before any focus on the pool of people we'll work alongside. This pool encompasses a diverse range of ages, life stages, personal values, political beliefs, and motivations. Such diversity provides distinct insights and context and introduces us to die-hard enthusiasts among passive-aggressive individuals. The spectrum can be wide. By this stage, we've likely developed strategies for working with diverse backgrounds, but the application of the three themes of "nurture, tolerate, or escalate" allows us to strategically approach these relationships.

In the sales arena, transitional relationships during our career years can become valuable leads for future sales opportunities. Consistent follow-ups and check-ins are crucial, acknowledging that while the initial relationship might be influenced by the professional environment, the long-term goal is to position oneself to assist in their future dreams and ambitions

When my dad first entered the insurance business four decades years ago, he approached some of his long-term friends not to try to sell them anything, but just to let them know that he had changed careers and now will offer financial services and insurance products and if they were ever in the market, he would be happy to visit with them. He did not try to sell his college friends or long-term high school friends, he just put it out there and said here's what he offers and let him know if they'd ever like to have a cup of coffee. His goal was to make his prospects into friends and clients and to *not* hound his friends into doing business with him because of years of transitional relationship. He did business with many friends from his youth who trusted him but more importantly trusted his process of transition-transaction-transformation.

Regardless of which arena or industry we work in, we may be forced to help people mature and grow up in their expectations.

Numerous success stories emerged from encounters in places like bible studies or the stranger next to him on the flight into Minneapolis from his latest business trip. Although many transitional relationships followed the patterns we described, my father also recognized the potential for relationships to form in unexpected places, such as an elevator ride spanning eight floors. This was his arena, and he was a natural in it. Rather than selling for the current reality, he sold for the next one. A delayed flight could lead to coffee, coffee could become a presentation, and that presentation could transform into a trusted advisory role over the years to come where he searched for all avenues to help clients plan for their next life stages.

His primary mantra was: "I have no reason to believe that you're in the market for the products and services I represent but I would like to show you the kind of work I do for my friends and clients. Would you have 30 minutes for a cup of coffee or tea?" His objective was to establish a professional, transactional relationship that could naturally evolve into a <u>transformational</u> one (we'll explore this later in the book, so stay tuned), without the entanglement of a myriad of products and transactions consumers encounter daily.

But how does this work with existing friendships? What about individuals we've known for a long time but never attempted to establish any form of business with them?

If you have established a long-term base with your prospects, a base that is founded on growing up together, going to college together, or going to church together it may be difficult to terminate the relationship when you no longer can provide value that will benefit them.

Often people do mature and grow up in their expectations. Some of my father's best business came from an organization and the CEO that he had worked with in a non-business setting for three years. When he initially approached the CEO about the opportunity to discuss how he serviced his clients, the CEO blew him off over a breakfast meeting. The CEO said he was satisfied with the company and representative and that there was no possibility of new business for my dad with him or his company. My dad said he would like to be in that enviable position one day and asked if they could just stay in touch and have breakfast on a frequent basis, during which time he could show him what he did for his clients and maybe he would know another organization that would benefit from his "transformational services".

Twenty years of coffee and breakfast together paid off as the CEO started to *trust* him with bits and pieces of the company's business. They are now doing what he promised; to maximize potential, minimize risk and manage future growth on all the mutual business they both desired.

When I entered industry, I was intrigued to discover that many accomplished sales professionals employed methods akin to my father's approach to generating leads. Embracing the current environment while considering the next one proved effective for all parties involved.

Are all stories like this? Definitely not. There will be instances when people resist change due to fear, loyalty to other providers, or a simple dislike for us and our approaches. Just as transitional relationships have a spectrum of outcomes, they also have varying levels of success.

Limited Selection Application

In the realm of consulting, many of these transitional relationships manifest as "stakeholders," the decision-makers assigned to collaborate with us. In the limited time we have in an assessment or engagement, our aim is to quickly nurture these relationships. These stakeholders could potentially become future clients as they transition to different companies or positions. Drawing from the research on "weak ties," a significant portion of our business referrals will come from these participants.

Nurturing must remain a priority.

Then there are individuals like "Frank," whom we encounter. According to Patrick Lencioni's book "The Ideal Team Player," Frank represents "The Skillful Politician" – someone who possesses hunger and intelligence but lacks humility (we highly recommend reading the book for a deeper understanding of these attributes). As we work closely with Frank, we may begin to perceive the backchannel maneuvering he engages in. Whether it's undermining our contributions or suggesting that the team's success isn't tied to our efforts, we've heard these sentiments before.

In such cases, we address the relationship from an escalation perspective. We attempt to tackle the behaviors and their corresponding outcomes head-on with Frank. While our primary scope doesn't involve professional relationship development or work ethic improvement, we find ourselves compelled to foster effective teamwork to accomplish our goals. However, working on behavior with Frank usually results in dismissive responses, ongoing political maneuvering (concurring with us but continuing back-channel activities), and rarely, actual change.

This marks the beginning of escalation to leadership. **Earlier in my career, I made the mistake of waiting too long to escalate such relationships.** Management wasn't pleased to learn that my reluctance to address team members' escalating behaviors led to missed deadlines, group-wide frustration, and poor performance down the line.

Determining when to escalate can vary and it primarily depends on the individuals involved, but each person should establish boundaries and adhere to them. One of the most frustrating situations is being told to *tolerate* a Frank.

This tolerance is rooted in the political dynamics that have existed in companies for centuries. Even after escalation, Frank remains unaltered. Frank's existence in the corporate world traces back to the industrial revolution and governmental policies aimed at rectifying its effects. Whether nepotism, equal employment, or prevailing compensation norms account for Frank's position, his approach continues unchanged. In such instances, we must focus on our decisions—whether to leave or stay—based on our emotional resilience and mental fortitude.

Tolerating a Frank often necessitates humility, confidence, and keeping future opportunities at the forefront of our minds. Countless athletes refer to this as "giving their all for the tape." While our environment may not resemble a championship setup, not exerting full effort during each encounter can result in documented shortcomings that are shared, analyzed, and might impact future opportunities. So, yes, tolerate, but also advocate for yourself.

An exciting facet of transitional relationships in careers is when transactional connections evolve into transitional ones. One of my favorite examples involves a friend that joined my old company as a project manager, and our interactions were initially transactional. He led most of the meetings my role and team supported. While he was driven and skilled, a discrepancy arose when he continued to push my team with a corporate agenda – an approach my team and I resisted as we preferred to execute things our way. After several months of tenses meetings and professional, yet unproductive communication, an external consultant advised me, "He's a good one, stay close with him." I acted on her advice, I invited him to a bowling night with a few colleagues. With the removal of the transactional aspect from our professional roles allowed us to view our coworkers as individuals rather than mere representatives of their departments or skills. He and I connected over college sports teams, hobbies, and shared life goals. While it wasn't instantaneous, our relationship transitioned to a more meaningful level as we aligned our corporate and personal objectives. We needed to take a deeper level or participation than just the acknowledgement that we each had roles that were part of a bigger story; it was about how we viewed each other as individuals with common aspirations. He provided insights into higher-level corporate objectives, and I introduced him to the frontline operators who were the driving force towards those goals. The transition elevated both of us, and our shared objectives shaped our growth and our families' journeys.

Other transitional relationships may not pose challenges as significant as a "Frank," but they can lead to frustrations in both professional and personal spheres. We can associate this category with "people pleasers," or individuals who offer responses aligned with their managers' preferences rather than expressing their genuine opinions. This isn't necessarily a negative experience, but it does create a drawback. The root of the frustration often lies in the extra time and effort required to achieve shared goals. Let's call these individuals "Kathy."

Kathy is on the team because of her opinions and knowledge, but sometimes her answers to questions do not fit the current situation but are aligned with the manager hypothetical solution. Kathy can be beneficial and productive to the team if she understands what's being "actually" stated in responding to hard questions asked of the team. When she provides the "right" answer without enough context, or the team's understanding, then a huge gap begins to evolve between the team and management.

You may argue that if Kathy knows the answer, then she has the context. You may be right, but I've met a lot of intelligent Kathy's that don't. This is demonstrated by the "book vs. street" knowledge. The book answer is what Kathy is providing, the street answer is what will make the goal achievable. It's providing "real" answers, based on more of the intangible items at play, and how they impact the question.

Offering clear answers that connect the dots between the response and the team's current environment is essential.

This might require humility, as well as the courage to confront complex questions with nuanced, real-world answers. Managers might keep pushing for easier solutions, but that's a different story that hinges on our ability to communicate effectively. Kathy can indeed be frustrating, but it's rarely her intention.

When *nurturing* Kathy, we should ask questions that seem simple. Encourage the team to explain the connections between their responses and the current environment.

Bring clarity to the situation.

This might be humbling, <u>but a competent manager will welcome this</u>, relieved to see effort invested in the pursuit of clarity. If a Kathy challenges the team's additional discussions, that's when the escalation conversation should begin. Remember, management isn't pleased to learn that we recognized a potential issue but hesitated to address it in the interest of avoiding conflict. We aren't expected to "fix" the reasons behind Kathy's responses. Our role with Kathy is to handle her within the categories we've defined (nurturing, escalating, or tolerating) and elevate mature relationships with her to the transformational stage, where we address behavior from that perspective.

Finally, I want to highlight a relationship that hasn't expired and continues to evolve. We met prior to "career" years" through church youth groups and stayed connected through college. After college we worked together for another five years and had a blast as we learned how industry worked, as well as how we grew in our personal lives. Throughout various transitional phases, our bond remained strong both in and outside of work. I'm grateful for him, his wife, and his role in introducing me to my wife and for the many shared experiences—weddings, football games, celebrating our children's birthdays, and providing unwavering support.

This relationship and others like it are worth highlighting because even if they don't evolve into transformational ones, they remain immensely meaningful and worth nurturing throughout life. The key is to stay connected through new transitional environments as we work toward common objectives, whether it's on the golf course or in the realm of parenthood. Continual change ensures that we don't become confined to reliving memories and the "good ole days" but rather continue creating new ones.

Let me conclude with a story about my father. He once met a restaurant owner during an afternoon coffee visit to the establishment. He knew that the owner was usually available for conversation around 2 PM on Tuesdays, my dad made it a habit to drop by. What began as a series of coffee chats eventually led to fruitful business interactions after three years. However, the real blessing was the 40-year friendship that blossomed from those Tuesday afternoons. Even when my father relocated a couple of years later, he made the effort, even if it meant a detour by 50 miles, to drive through town for coffee and meaningful conversations.

CHAPTER 6

Transitional Relationships–2nd Stage Years

Transitional Paths

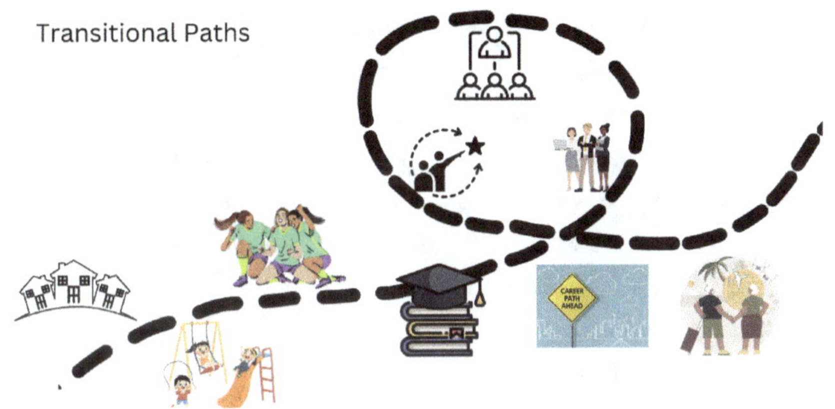

James Johnson >> *I deeply admire Josiah's perspective on handling most of these topics. However, experience and age provide me with insights that Josiah might not fully grasp at this point. With that in mind, I'd like to delve into the next category of transitional relationships, which Josiah might not relate to for some time. Let me summarize what happens to relationships that never progressed into transformation or were introduced to me in my current retirement phase.*

Consider what occurs with relationships involving old bosses, employers, neighbors, or childhood friends once you've moved on. Given the preva-

lence of email and social media, it's hard to disconnect entirely. We seem to stay superficially "connected" through holiday cards or other low-effort interactions. The defining characteristic of this category is that time becomes a dominant factor, outweighing the impact of the environment. In this context, dedicating time to nurturing new relationships might not be a priority. Even maintaining existing non-transformative relationships tends to take a backseat.

So, what did I do when I retired and essentially shifted around 400 relationships from a mindset of nurturing, caring, and transformation to a more relaxed "how are you doing" approach?

I allowed these relationships to run on "cruise control" and redirected my focus towards certain transactional friendships and connections. These are individuals I've always enjoyed conversations with or the occasional cup of coffee, but I no longer need to concern myself with the minutiae that were crucial during my career years when I attempted to transform the relationship. These interactions are now guided by a shared desire to share life experiences and relate to each other's present realities, irrespective of our career paths. There's no need to deliberate over whether to nurture or escalate these relationships. Worries about learning "bad habits" from this group simply do not arise.

I find myself dedicating time to reconnect with many of my former clients and transitional relationships from my years in sales, without the pressure of needing to close a deal. Instead, our focus shifts towards who will emerge victorious in the next round of mini-golf or planning for the upcoming vacation.

CHAPTER 7

Transformational Relationships

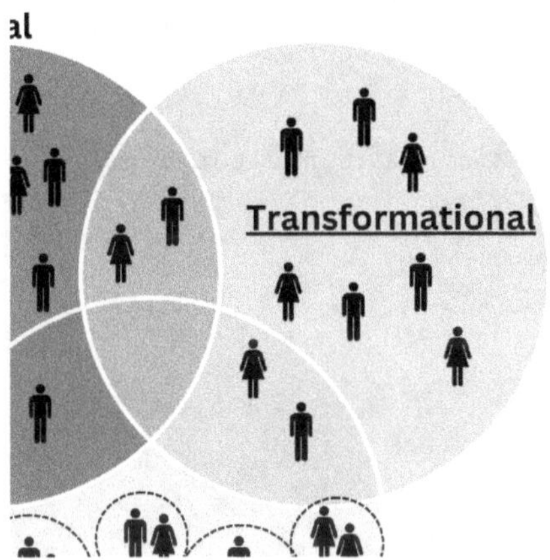

We arrive at the ultimate relationship. A type of relationship that is based on where they may take us. These relationships provide mutual growth and make us better than the people we were when we first entered into them.

This relationship is looking for the same thing a caterpillar is looking for when it spins a cocoon. It's the desire for a dramatic change, a transformation, <u>to become something that you never could have become if you stayed in the other two stages of relationship that we have discussed.</u>

You are transformed by renewing or changing of your mind.

This pertains to us, our circumstances, and those we are connected with. Instead of viewing people as "a means to an end," we now recognize them as the outcome of our efforts, actions, and existence.

This category of relationships may only make up around 20% of our relationships but they will require about 80% of our effort in maintaining them. The advantage is that this will come naturally as these relationships are with people we love being around because they make us better (wives, best friends, mentees spending time with their mentors). The challenge and where there will be consistent struggle is in the prioritization of time, no matter how few there may be to maintain.

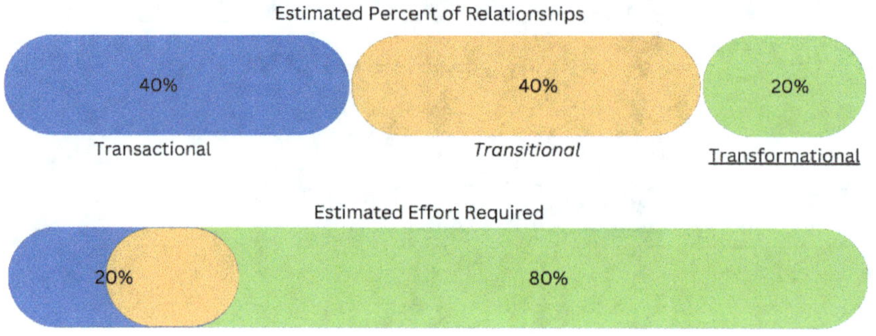

It's remarkable how the attitudes of prospects, suspects, customers, clients, friends, and acquaintances change when we understand they are part of our life story to help us achieve our goals and fulfill our professional mission by assisting them in reaching their objectives. Throughout our experience in the marketplace, recruiting, training, and selling, we've observed that success is limited when transformation isn't the primary goal, both personally and corporately.

We've said it, and we'll say it again. Transformational relationships are born when we help another become someone they never could have become without our interaction, and we become someone that we never would have become without their investment in us.

Natural Selection

Life's pivotal relationships often require some form of natural selection before we identify them as significant. Some of these connections emerge during times of change, while others happen by chance or are seen as part of a greater design leading us to converge. Regardless of how they come about, the essential factors remain: being in the right location, with the right individual, at the perfect moment.

Grow where you are planted.

We might bump into potential partners anytime, so it's important to be ready to see how those relationships could turn out. This applies not just at work but also in our private lives, even though the way we assess them might change depending on the situation. The real value of these connections is found in having meaningful discussions and pushing each other's viewpoints. If someone doesn't know what they stand for or can't express it, the benefits of the relationship drop significantly.

Before we expand more into the criteria, it's imperative to acknowledge that the individuals involved in such a relationship are rooted in certain core beliefs that shape their worldview. These foundational beliefs encompass various aspects including finances, religion, ethics, sexuality, politics, media preferences, parenting philosophies, occupation, and education, among others. While the essence of a transformational relationship lies in the renewal or alteration of one's mindset, if an individual's core beliefs remain shallow, they can dilute the value of their counterpart's contributions. In such cases, discussions tend to revolve around agreements rather than raising deeper internal debates on important subjects.

In simpler terms, when an individual lacks clarity about their own convictions, it places an undue burden on the other party to steer the conversation and relationship.

The subsequent criteria are precisely that—benchmarks to consider when assessing whether a relationship holds the potential for transformation. However, they should not be mistaken for the sole ingredients necessary to cultivate a transformational relationship.

<u>*Overall Qualifier:*</u>

1. *Do I trust this person, and do they know what I'm looking for?*
   1. *Transformational relationships are reliant upon trust.*

<u>*Personal Relationship*</u>

1. *Will I have enough context to connect with this person?*
   1. *Transformational relationships are dependent upon relatable context.*

<u>*Professional Relationship*</u>

1. *Does their work ethic resemble the same high standard that I strive for?*
   1. *Transformational relationships thrive when assistance can be provided based upon experienced practices.*

These are the base starting points for qualifying a relationship, but in the end, it's routed in the same, core goal:

Transformational relationships are born when we help another become someone they never could have become without our interaction, and we become someone that we never would have become without their investment in us

When seeking individuals for transformative relationships, faith-based or departmental small groups are fantastic starting points for finding people who share your goals and beliefs, and more importantly, a mutual desire to grow. These groups help highlight essential qualifications; however, when examined individually, these traits take on even greater significance.Being part of a purpose-driven small group, alongside the regularity of meetings (cadence), ensures accountability towards those internal goals. This dynamic is crucial for the group's effectiveness, and it's apparent how any misalignment can lead to a significant loss of value.Now, let's zoom in on one-on-one relationships. The consistency of interaction (cadence) and the shared sense of accountability play vital roles in enhancing the relationship's efficiency. However, if the core elements lack clarity or alignment, progress stalls. In such relationships built on trust, this mutual accountability becomes increasingly evident.

In his book "Trust" by Henry Cloud, he explores the importance of living in alignment with truth and the consequences of avoiding or distorting it. Cloud highlights how truth serves as the foundation for healthy relationships, personal growth, and overall well-being. He emphasizes that embracing truth requires courage and vulnerability, as it often involves facing difficult realities and acknowledging our own limitations.

Cloud delves into various aspects of trust, such as the power of truth-telling and the necessity of establishing boundaries to protect ourselves from falsehoods. He emphasizes the importance of surrounding ourselves with truth-tellers who can provide honest feedback and challenge our perspectives, helping us to grow and improve.

Furthermore, Cloud discusses the damaging effects of lies, deception, and denial, which can lead to broken trust, strained relationships, and personal stagnation. He encourages readers to confront their own tendencies to avoid or distort the truth, offering practical strategies for embracing truthfulness and fostering a culture of honesty in our lives.

In essence, "Trust" serves as a guide for individuals seeking personal growth, stronger relationships, and a more fulfilling life by embracing the transformative power of truth and living authentically. That's why trust is at the core of being a qualifier for this type of relationship.

Champion Mindset

Another trait to consider for transformational relationships, is what we refer to as the "champion mindset". In contrast to the cheerleading mentality that we discussed in the transitional relationships, the champion mindset may not be all that positive in some circumstances. The champion knows what it takes to succeed, to win, and to move on to the next goal.

At the most intense level, Admiral James Stockdale understood this concept and it became known as "The Stockdale Paradox". Stockdale was a prisoner of war during the Vietnam War. It refers to the idea of maintaining a balance between optimism and realism in challenging situations. Admiral Stockdale survived his ordeal by embracing two key beliefs: an unwavering faith in his eventual rescue and a confrontational acknowledgment of the harsh realities of his captivity.

The Stockdale Paradox suggests that a champion mindset involves having a strong vision and unwavering confidence in achieving success, while also maintaining a clear-eyed view of the current circumstances and potential obstacles.

The Stockdale Paradox

It's about finding the balance between optimism and realism. Champions understand the importance of setting high goals and maintaining a positive mindset, but they also recognize the need to face and overcome challenges. In practical terms, the Stockdale Paradox can be applied by acknowledging and accepting the difficulties and setbacks that may arise in the pursuit of success, while still maintaining an unwavering belief in one's abilities and the ultimate achievement of the desired outcome. It's about staying committed, resilient, and adaptable in the face of adversity, while remaining optimistic and focused on the long-term goal.

Ultimately, a champion mindset combines optimism and realism, allowing individuals to navigate challenges with determination, perseverance, and a belief in their own abilities. By embracing the Stockdale

Paradox, individuals can cultivate the mental fortitude and resilience necessary to overcome obstacles and achieve greatness.

In the transformational relationship, we are looking for, and rely on the other participant to help us focus on our destination while providing their thoughts on any realities we are in.

Maintenance is Key

Ever wonder why keeping up with yards, gardens, old cars, or any mechanical stuff takes up so much time and effort? I sure have. While I'm not completely sure why it feels this way, I've noticed that skipping maintenance usually makes things a lot worse. My daughters and I learn this lesson every summer when we set up our above-ground pool and start filling it up. Even though we try hard to skim the water, shower before swimming, and use shock treatments, our nice little oasis often turns into a green-tinged swamp. Fixing the water ends up taking more time and energy than we even want to spend on swimming in the first place.

This recurring experience underscores the undeniable truth: **consistent maintenance is the cornerstone of long-term sustainment.**

It's an interesting thought—if we take the time to maintain both living and non-living things, why wouldn't we do the same for our relationships? Keeping our connections strong is essential for really enjoying and benefiting from them. Even though it might feel unnecessary during those nostalgic moments with friends and family, its importance can't be overstated. Whether these experiences become truly impactful depends on a few factors. We often think back to times that bring a flood of nostalgia, reminding us of the beginnings of our bonds. These moments have a special charm, but they also show when a relationship no longer fits who we've become, which can feel a bit awkward.While the emotions and memories tied to the past are wonderful, they don't make a relationship transformative by themselves. Even if slipping back into those old dynamics feels easy, if there's a weak link between past and present, real change can't happen. But when the connection is strong, the need for maintenance becomes obvious.

Maintenance sets up how the rhythm of interaction and mutual responsibility work between people. In personal relationships, this structure is usually more laid-back, while in professional ones, it tends to be formal. No matter the style, understanding how deep and intense the relationship might get is key.

Cadence	**Accountability**
Weekly	**Guardrails**
Monthly	**Screening**
Ad-hoc	**Phone-a-friend**

Having a good rhythm and accountability plan makes things easier to maintain—it's really that simple. When we talk about cadence, we're just referring to how often we meet. Just set up a meeting schedule and stick to it. If things change, tweak the timing to keep everything running smoothly.

Accountability shows up differently depending on the relationship, but in transformative ones, it might mean helping each other set boundaries, joining in decision-making processes, or being that go-to person for advice. These practices tend to be pretty flexible.

It necessitates both participants understanding each other's aspirations and objectives thoroughly, enabling them to collaboratively shape these mechanisms.

Once this transparency and mutual understanding are established, they become the benchmark for accountability between the two transformed individuals. In essence: we collectively agreed that either you or I would work toward a particular (professional or personal) goal, and the current opportunity or circumstance is either aligned with that trajectory or not. This process becomes notably more manageable when the objectives are clearly outlined, which offers a significant advantage, given that these discussions usually involve intricate considerations in determining the right path forward.

Guardrails

I first encountered the concept of relational guardrails when my father gave me a book by Andy Stanley, a well-known pastor and author. Stanley introduces "guardrails" as principles or boundaries that protect us from the negative effects of our decisions and actions. Similar to how guardrails on the road provide some leeway before reaching danger, relationship guardrails should offer some buffer before serious issues arise, causing minor inconvenience as a warning.Here are key points from Stanley's teaching on guardrails:

Define Your Personal Guardrails: Stanley stresses the importance of proactively setting personal guardrails to guide behavior. These moral and ethical boundaries help us make prudent choices and avoid situations that could lead to adverse outcomes.

Learn from Your Past Mistakes: Reflecting on past errors and using them as learning experiences is crucial. By recognizing past difficulties or poor decisions, we can establish guardrails to prevent similar mistakes in the future.

Use External Guardrails: Besides personal guidelines, external guardrails, such as the counsel and influence of trusted friends, mentors, or accountability partners, are vital. Their advice helps us make better decisions and stay on track.

Establish Guardrails in Key Areas: Focusing on specific areas where boundaries are essential, like relationships, finances, work-life balance, and personal habits, can shield us from potential harm or negative consequences.

Embrace Grace and Flexibility: While guardrails are important, so is grace and adaptability. We are imperfect and will sometimes make mistakes or stray off course. It's important to grant ourselves and others grace and to adjust our guardrails if needed.

Guardrails Promote Freedom: Contrary to the belief that guardrails limit freedom, Stanley argues they actually enhance it. Boundaries create safety and protection, allowing us to make wise choices and pursue our goals confidently without fearing disastrous outcomes.

Overall, Andy Stanley emphasizes the necessity of setting personal and external boundaries to safeguard ourselves from negative effects. By defining guardrails, learning from past experiences, seeking advice, and establishing boundaries in crucial areas, we can make wiser decisions and achieve greater freedom in our lives. Developing these up front in transformational relationships might require initial effort but promises long-term benefits with minimal ongoing maintenance.

Screening

Screening can be a concurrent process, either alongside established guardrails or independently from them. The screening involves the very discussions we previously mentioned – those instances when we face novel opportunities or situations, seeking sagacity and direction that aligns with our objectives. When guardrails are not in place, we rely on our transformational champion to fulfill the role we delineated. They assist us in assessing or mentoring the various approaches to the immediate circumstances and how these align with our goals. The underlying notion here is that these conversations are anticipatory and forward-looking.

Regrettably, in many transitional or transactional relationships, these conversations often occur post facto – <u>after</u> a decision has been made or an occurrence has reached its resolution. They become tales to share or experiences to pass on. In transformational relationships, we ought to be prompt in engaging these discussions *before* they solidify into narratives.

This might even serve as a method for discerning the optimal solution: by pondering, "How would I like to recount this tale someday?" and inviting the champion to scrutinize the narrative against the broader objectives while considering external factors.

The ultimate goal is to assess potential choices and situations from a proactive standpoint, rather than merely reacting to them once they've transpired. By involving the transformational champion in this evaluation process, the relationship becomes an instrument for refining decisions and embracing opportunities that align more effectively with our overarching aspirations.

Transformational relationships should be depended upon to help us screen decisions <u>before</u> they become our stories.

Then there is the least desired accountability plan, but necessary for our humanistic selves, the reactionary response.

Phone-A-Friend

Depending on our life stage, we've likely found ourselves on both ends of a practice that has a certain notoriety—the dreaded phone call. It's a call we're all familiar with, and it's not the exhilarating unexpected call we might be hoping for. These calls emerge from a mentee, a child, a partner, or a close colleague. Typically, they transpire exclusively within transformational relationships, although this wasn't used as a criterion since we prefer to avoid the negativity that often accompanies these calls.

The sequence is familiar:
A situation arises...

...A decision is made...
...A misstep takes place*...
...A goal may be in jeopardy...

I've certainly made my share of such calls to my father and a few other pivotal relationships. The asterisk next to "A misstep took place" is intentional; in my experience, the perceived misstep wasn't always significant, yet the sentiment was consistent. These calls can be demanding, but their significance is evident. As their champion, your role transcends that of a mere cheerleader. You've aligned with them on their objectives and dreams, and now they perceive they've fallen short. In such moments, there's a variety of ways to handle the call, but brevity is key. It could be as simple as stating, "What's done is done; now, what's our plan moving forward?" The ultimate resolution might not be reached during the call, but the tone is set, evoking the essence of the Stockdale Paradox. Once realigned with the recalibrated path, it's imperative to redirect focus toward reevaluating the maintenance strategy to prevent future calls of this nature.

This accountability practice, or rather, the absence of productivity in the initial two practices, underscores why we emphasize not allowing mismatched transitional relationships to progress and advocate for patient evaluation of potential relationships over an extended period. This "Phone-A-Friend" scenario can be draining under certain circumstances. When a participant isn't interested in upfront maintenance but instead seeks a crutch in the form of a brief phone call to address their current predicament, it proves detrimental to all parties involved.

While my father and I lack the expertise to fully grasp the emotional and cognitive intricacies at play within these relationships, we acknowledge their existence, shaped by diverse factors unique to each individual. As more children and adults are increasingly turning to therapists and psychologists, the potential benefits are immense. For the purpose of this book, such support may even foster healthier, transformational relationships.

There might arrive a point when a transformational relationship needs to reach its conclusion. We've explored where a relationship shouldn't have been perceived as transformational from the outset. That's one end of the spectrum. However, there could also be instances where the demands of maintenance and accountability become overwhelming for one of the participants. In either scenario, ending such a relationship is undeniably challenging. It's not advisable to adopt the approach often seen in transactional relationships – simply walking away.

The difficulty lies in processing the unfulfilled potential that lingers. It's a potential that may never be fully realized. This can strike at the very core of our being particularly if we held the other participant's influence in high esteem, or viewed it as pivotal in our journey to become the person we aspired to be.

Depending on the setting of the relationship there may be additional repercussions than just processing end of the relationship:

participants may look for new careers,
search out new industries to target,
readjust their field of study,
choose to move out...

When a transformational relationship becomes one-sided, the resulting sense of loss can be profound, akin to mourning the end of something cherished. In some cases, processing these emotions might even necessitate therapy to navigate the complexities involved.

During the decision-making process to end such a relationship, the same tactics that originally formed the connection can be useful.

1. Engage in in-depth discussions about shared goals
2. Reference the context in which the relationship was formed

3. Reflect on the mutual trust and influence or
4. Address the skills you aspired to acquire that were modeled by the other participant.

Through these conversations, it's possible to assess whether the one-sided nature is a result of changed circumstances for one or both parties or if the relationship genuinely lacks balance.

While we hope this situation never arises, it's important to acknowledge that the aspiration for transformational relationships with close friends and family can make such situations more likely. Although not easy, ending a one-sided relationship is valuable for the betterment of your future self.

Draw to a Close

As with many principles and structures, there exist potential exceptions that may either apply to all criteria discussed or none at all. Herein lies a potential loophole – some transformational relationships don't adhere to the concept of "maintenance" while also not fitting the criteria for transitional relationships. In these cases, there might not be an active environment where both participants can engage, yet elements such as shared goals, skills, and context don't necessarily require ongoing upkeep. Think of past mentors, former bosses, distant colleagues, instructors, or close friends who moved away.

Despite the lack of active engagement, we still view these relationships as transformational in nature because the champion mindset and trust endure. The key difference is that the practical application might not be readily feasible. These relationships often grow in number and value over time, reflecting themes akin to the "2nd Stage." The distinguishing factor is that a transformative impact did occur at some point; the connection was pivotal in both individuals' growth into transformed beings. This quality is one that is rarely allowed to come to an end.

Transformational Innovation

Through our thorough examination of methods to cultivate these relationships, a recurring and seemingly straightforward answer consistently emerges. Yet, this answer is often one of the most challenging aspects to accumulate as we age: time and energy. As a millennial, I've encountered my fair share of wisdom through memes. One such visual presented a venn diagram illustrating the balance between time, energy, and money. I've adjusted this concept to align with the themes we've explored in our categories.

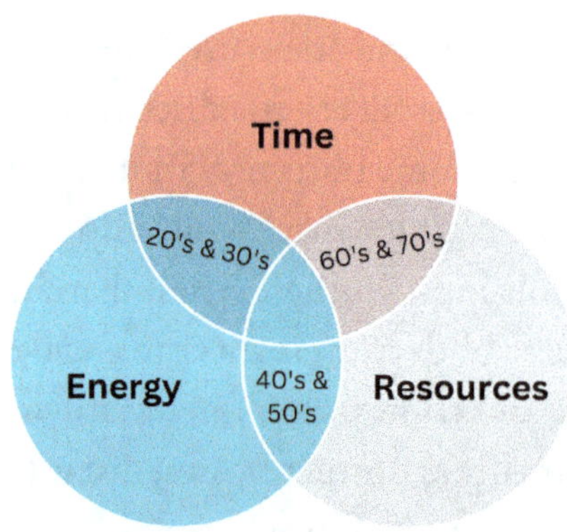

The diagram illustrates how in our 20-30's we have time and energy, but not much money. Later, during our 40's and 50's we have energy and money, but lack time. Finally in the later years we have time and money but not energy.

Transformational relationships cannot be bought, so that's why it's critical to select and nurture these relationships when time and energy is readily available (in our 20-30's). As we age we'll need to allocate precious time to these relationships (many of these may be within your household with your significant others and children) and later we'll have to devote any energy available to these.

Time and energy are precious assets that can't be fabricated or saved up. It's essential to wisely distribute our limited resources with intention.

The best way to succeed is by prioritizing with intention. You may find that you can only genuinely invest in one or two transformative relationships each month, and that's completely fine. This needs to be a key part of your ongoing efforts. At times, it might seem like the same two relationships are your main focus every single month for an entire year. That's just how life goes, and our task is to keep prioritizing effectively. We must bring intentionality to the time and energy we dedicate to these relationships. Even in our conversations, we cannot let distractions pull us away from maintaining a 100% commitment to a champion mindset.By doing this, we tap into the most fulfilling elements of these connections. Grounded in core values such as trust, common objectives, skills, and shared context, these relationships offer a rich environment for meaningful and challenging dialogues. In these conversations, questions like "Do you truly believe that?" and "What's driving your thinking?" become more than just remarks—they spark deep explorations of important matters. This grants us the liberty to discuss topics that might feel awkward elsewhere because both people share these foundational values. While aligned on values, each person brings their unique perspective, fostering vibrant discussions to understand those values in depth. The journey features two inquisitive minds reshaping their thoughts in innovative ways. It's akin to the intellectual debates Socrates and other Greek philosophers had long ago, but now with the added benefit of endless discussion topics easily found through social media scrolling.

Whether the topics at hand involve faith, finance, politics, parenting, historical interpretations, or the meanings behind literature, these discussions hold genuine significance. They establish the foundation for the more consequential, accountability-driven conversations. In manufacturing, the term "fire-fighting" refers to addressing issues as they arise rather than focusing on long-term, systemic solutions. This analogy can be applied to the maintenance aspect of transformational relationships. However, our ultimate goal is to spend time cultivating enduring, systemic goals and aspirations within each other. This approach leads to reduced instances of firefighting and grants us more opportunities to engage in enjoyable coffee conversations, much like the ones my father and I relish.

Transformed Souls

Quick note before going into the examples of some of our transformational relationships. We tried to develop the key characteristic or trait that we admired and wanted to learn how to replicate in our own lives. The traits themselves are unique to the people in the relationship. This is not examples to say what specific types of traits you should be looking for in a transformational relationship, only that they exist. The remaining transformational themes of champion mindset, shared context, trust, etc.... may or may not be shared depending on the individual but they exist. Now enjoy taking a peak into our transformed souls.

Highschool Beginnings

One of the most enduring transformational relationships I've been fortunate enough to nurture began during an unexpected summer camp experience. I met Joel W at Covenant Park Bible Camp and what initially transpired in a transient setting soon evolved into a profound connection. As two young men navigating the complexities of high school, we forged a bond that transcended the camp's temporary environment. Despite attending different high schools, we found common ground in each other's kitchens, surrounded by family and friends. Our shared knowledge of the tastiest treats hidden in cupboards solidified our brotherly connection. While there were consistent few of us hanging out, it was Joel's exceptional loyalty that set him apart. His loyalty never wavered and is a trait deeply ingrained in his character. I could always count on him; he was a man of his word.

Though stubbornness played a role, his commitment to trustworthiness and loyalty was undeniable. Initially I had determined to embark on my college journey independently, but Joel's suggestion to explore his chosen school changed my perspective. The idea of navigating those initial college years alongside a close friend appealed to me, and it proved to be a rewarding decision.

Throughout our college journey, we supported each other in our progression to graduate and experience life to the fullest. Looking back, I'm amuse that while we held each other to such high standards, we (primarily myself) hesitated to reach out for help when facing challenges, fearing judgment. Over time, we grasped the true essence of loyalty, and that it meant being there for one another, even during the toughest times. We've stood by each other in weddings, have become uncles to each other's daughters, and remained staunch advocates for each other's growth. Joel is a remarkably humble and genuine individual and to have witnessed the twists and turns in our personal and professional lives has been remarkable. Despite life's changes, we continue to play pivotal roles in each other's unfolding chapters.

Around the same time I met Joel, I met another transformative friendship I forged was with Austin J. Austin stood out as one of the loudest, most playful 17-year-olds in our high school. Yet, beneath the noise and jest, lay a self-assured man ready to tackle any challenge. He was unafraid to voice his opinions, regardless of the context or subject. Before I met Austin, I was rather reserved and spent a significant amount of time behind a computer to connect with friends through AIM and Facebook. Austin, in his distinct way, pointed out the inadequacy of this approach and encouraged me to be more actively engaged in social circles in person. He introduced me (sometimes against my will) to various social groups, led me to meet more people in two months than I had in the previous two years of high school. While I initially believed that everyone liked Austin, I eventually learned that his demeanor didn't always win everyone over. However, what set Austin apart was his indifference to others' opinions – he remained true to himself, unaffected by how others perceived him.

This was a life-changing revelation for someone like me, who often tried to fit in and be liked by everyone, especially figures of authority. Austin taught me that while respect is essential, allowing it to change who we are is another matter entirely.

After graduation, Austin was called to California, where he pursued his personal legend (Austin is, in my view, a living embodiment of

Santiago from "The Alchemist," despite never having read the book). His journey was marked by trials, successes, failures, and challenges. Throughout it all, he maintained an unshakable belief in his ability to succeed, regardless of present circumstances. Whenever I visited him or we spoke on the phone, our conversations carried an undercurrent of challenge. We live very different lives, and to an outsider, it might even seem unlikely that we're as close as we are.

Despite these differences, our dialogues are characterized by this ongoing challenge – questions about each other's lives. "That sounds like a great professional achievement, but how is your family? How are they feeling?" or "This seems like a comfortable situation, but what's next? How will it become exceptional?" We know that the other person has the answer, yet we continue to pose the question.

Between these two relationships that began in high school and continue to thrive, there's no doubt that without them, I wouldn't have become the person I believe I was destined to be. Nor would I be living a life that I truly love.

Professional Mentors

I hadn't heard about the Gallup Strength finder exercise or reports, nor what the themes were, but once I learned that my boss at the time, Rick H, had "Developer", I wasn't surprised. Gallup describes it as:

"People exceptionally talented in the Developer theme recognize and cultivate the potential in others. They spot the signs of each small improvement and derive satisfaction from evidence of progress".

The third "origin story" I'm about to share is particularly relevant to the book's themes, and it centers around my relationship with Rick. Our initial interaction occurred during the Valet years, a phase I referred to earlier when discussing transactional relationships. Rick was a hotel guest who stayed at the hotel while he prepared to move his family to Duluth for a new job. Our interactions were simple but genuine, characterized by meaningful conversations whenever they occurred. Rick's interest was further piqued when he learned about my academic background.

During the fall semester of my junior year, I received a call from Rick. He invited me to tour the manufacturing plant where he was employed the next time I was home. Although I was already employed as a full-time intern at another manufacturing plant in Rochester, Minnesota, I welcomed the opportunity. The tour was eye-opening, and it revealed Rick's extensive knowledge and made it clear that he would be an excellent mentor. While I wanted to change my employment right there on the spot, I didn't. While I felt a sense of missed opportunity due to that commitment, Rick and I agreed to stay connected.

My experience in Rochester didn't unfold as I had envisioned. The realization that it wasn't the right fit began to take hold during my annual trip to Las Vegas with my father in March. Over numerous discussions and debates about my options and future, my dad encouraged me to reach out to Rick. Upon my return, I called Rick and together we formulated a plan for me to work with him that summer.

This marked the point at which Rick's developer skills came to the forefront, and I assumed the role of his student. Right from the start, he bridged the gap between the technical and theoretical knowledge I had acquired and its practical implementation in the industry. Rick not only gave me opportunities to showcase my skills within the larger team but also shared with me the profound wisdom behind effective manufacturing methods – the people factor.

Rick's achievements were founded and based on his ability to construct teams of talented individuals matched with meaningful opportunities. Over the years, as I honed this skill, my relationship with Rick evolved into a transformational one that transcended the workplace. Rick, along with a few others, began joining my father and I on our Vegas trips. He became a staunch supporter and champion within the professional realm and emerged as a trusted friend and mentor on a personal level.

Life also as a funny way of intertwining great relationships as Rick and Joel eventually had conversations during some group hangouts which eventually culminated in the establishment of a brewery, rooted in their shared philosophy of creating teams that combine talent with valuable opportunities.

Rick wasn't the only key relationship I met at that initial manufacturing tour. Rick introduced me to another integral team member, Herbie D. Our bond was immediately established when, during my second week under his leadership, I boldly requested a day off to redeem a coupon for 18 holes of golf that was about to expire. As an avid golfer himself, Herbie understood my perspective, and we embarked on numerous rounds of golf. Through these shared experiences on the golf course, our relationship underwent a profound transformation. Our conversations ranged from lighthearted topics like the unlikely prospects of Minnesota producing a championship sports team, to more serious matters, including workplace challenges and even personal hardships that society often deems off-limits for discussion. Herbie and I navigated all these aspects together, sharing our lives in their entirety.

The quality that stands out prominently and that Herbie imparted to me is perseverance. It's the determination to navigate the unpolished aspects of life. The growth we both experienced during our relationship can be attributed to this quality. I've witnessed countless instances where Herbie could have chosen the path of self-preservation when confronted with tough decisions. Yet, that's not in his character. He consistently chooses what's right, even when he's exceptionally challenged in the moment.

He might not think people are observing, but they are, and that very perseverance is why I've always wanted him by my side, and vice versa. Whether in work or personal matters, whenever I contemplated taking an easier route that led astray, Herbie was quick to guide me back and stand shoulder-to-shoulder in the struggle. Occasionally, we reminisce about who we were when we first met, reflecting on the journey we've undertaken. Despite the hardships, we recognize that each of us played a crucial role in the other's growth and how it shaped us into individuals who wouldn't wish for anything to be different.

Dependable teammates

It's only fitting that my last two transformational relationship examples fit in the same category as I've met them both around the same time, and the three of us were part of the vows on my wedding day. Let me explain...

During my first consulting days, I was a single late 20-something excited to travel and see what industry was all about. A couple months after I joined another similar aged man joined the practice, who was married with a 6-month-old girl. We were both candidates for two new projects starting up.

Option 1: Spend 3-weeks at a time in Sweden at a manufacturing plant, with the opportunity for cheap European travel on the weekends

Option 2: Spend 15 hours each week to commute to and from northern New York that consisted of at least 2 plane connection (there was also a car-ferry requirement in there) to work in a secluded office doing excel all day...

To my knowledge I still don't know how or why I wasn't able to galivant around northern Europe for a couple months, but all I know is that I did not like Steven B, because he was selected for that option. We both ended up being successful in the projects yet for the next 6 months I didn't want anything to do with the guy who took my opportunity.

That was until he called me and offered an opportunity to join his project down in Florida during the cold Minnesota winters. Steven had started to turn the corner in my book. Through the next couple weeks, we started to really connect on the professional front, and then it transformed into the personal side.

From the time of my missed Scandinavian adventure, I had met and developed a relationship with my future wife. During my discussions with steven, I had started to think seriously about next steps with Grethell and what that meant for me and her two daughters. I needed a sounding board. Steven was about to welcome his new son into the world in a couple weeks, so our conversations got "real" quick. I was young and naïve when it came to understanding the full weight of dating a single mother. I had an idea of what it was supposed to mean, but that might have been from the movies.

Steven stressed to me the <u>responsibility</u> that I was about to take on. As a married man, as a father symbol, as a male in an interracial couple. It was Steven's ability to help coach me from his own raw experiences that provided me with the proper context to apply to my own home life. These girls won't be my blood but the role that I'll need to play doesn't care about blood.

As March of 2020 entered our lives, so did lock-downs, quarantines and the tragic George Floyd killing. My application to this new knowledge was about to be put to the test. Grethell, the girls, and I (our "new" family) grew even closer during that time rather than let any of those events drive us apart and that was a result of Steven's coaching. I had many responsibilities to my family whether I had chosen all of them or not didn't matter.

It is on the topic of responsibility to our family and careers that keep our conversations going on our typical Friday afternoon phone call. We discuss ideas such as "how much time can you be away from home before it begins skirting the responsibility of supporting what is happening <u>at</u> home". Keep in mind, Steven, myself and the rest of our peers spend about 175 nights in hotel rooms on the road each year... that's well over half of our time away from missing bedtimes, the dinner time tantrums, the early morning rushes... where does our responsibility land on those fronts?

Where is our responsibility in providing enough for our families to achieve the lives we see for them, to expand our children's view on life beyond what is currently available to them, to make sure they are cared for. How should we interpret our responsibility when it comes to our own God given passions for racing, golf, and the hectic and stressful jobs that we know and love and know that another career may not provide us the same satisfaction. Steven and I continue to be candid on these topics with one another because we are aligned on what one another wants out of this thing called life.

It makes the accountability portion of transformational relationships easy as I described. We are laser focused on the target but need to account for these items in the periphery.

This deep routed sense of responsibility found in Steven makes the next story almost anti-climactic. Grethell and I were 6 months out from our wedding, and we had wrapped up our premarital counseling with the Pastor when a new detour got introduced. He couldn't be available the day of our wedding.

After we got over the initial surprise, Grethell and I developed a decent plan: We both loved Steven's humor, Steven's a good speaker, Steven gets us. Conclusion: let's have Steven "host the wedding". Whether our plan was "legal" or not, we asked Steven if he would be host and coordinate the vows while I figured out who could sign the wedding certificate, or whether we would be married prior to the ceremony. The next day, as I reached out to a couple signature designees, but then I received an ordained certificate, or whatever the requirement is, from Steven who had jumped on the task the night before and figured out all the requirements necessary to marry us on our special day.

Responsibility. Steven wasn't going to allow anyone else to disrupt him from what he planned to do and he answered the call like a transformational friend.

Now for the beautiful one that was standing up there with Steven and myself; my stunning wife Grethell. The first time I met my wife was in 5th grade or so when we were in summer theater camp together. No, this won't be a story of elementary sweethearts that stayed together all through high school and early 20's. Our connection was peak transitional relationship and once the camp ended, my summer crush disappeared. That disappearance act worked for the next 20 years until we discovered one another again through some friends.

In that time, we had very different experiences that made the alignment of our paths an impossible task on paper. When we did rekindle, we met through some friends, and after we talked for a bit, I quickly stated "Well I'm back to my home in Alabama next week" as I was only home to see my parents when we met. It didn't scare her off at first but I thought that it would only be another transitional relationship with unrealized potential. We kept in touch via texts, phone calls and post-cards as I worked across the US at different clients. (I keep the tradition alive for my post-card worthy destinations).

In those messages I started to learn more about my future wife, and noticed she demonstrated a trait that I valued. **Resilience**. Whether out of need or desire, she had wielded this power in overcoming any setback that she has experienced.

This woman is a fierce warrior, and so are her daughters. I noticed it early on in how she had talked about her experiences during the 20 years of not being on my radar. She gave birth to two beautiful girls and pursued her nursing degree as they were toddlers. Confronted the struggles of a divorce, restarted life as a single mother in a small apartment... this woman had survived. It was in our discussions of how we overcame challenges where I knew I wanted to have her by my side and continue to transform me as much as I could transform her.

Grethell and I are dreamers at heart. We both continue to cast visions of what we want to do and who we want to be two, five, and ten years from now. We discuss what kind of life do we want to provide for our girls Ezra and Annorah. We do that together and establish the "guardrails" in how we are going to achieve it. We allow each other to pursue their passion, as long as it's in line with the destination. We haven't had the "phone-a-friend" call due to this. Through different career changes, health concerns, financial worries, 175+ nights on the road, pre-teen girl challenges, we let the guardrails provide the path to stay on track. If we ever get too close to the edge, we pause and allow our resilience to provide the pulse of getting back on track.

"The most important part of pressing pause, is hitting play again"

This was our motto when Grethell's heart stopped multiple times for fifteen seconds one evening while fast asleep. We were petrified of that realization the next day when the hospital called with the news (they had monitored her heart for a couple weeks). One micro-pacemaker and "routine" heart surgery later, she now has a constant reminder of a battery in her giving her a little shock back to life.

It was though this, while she recovered on the very floor where she was a cardiac nurse, that she agreed that it wasn't going to stop her from living life to the fullest. These literal and figurative pauses have defined our lives not by the situation, but how we have responded to them.

CHAPTER 8

Parenting Relationships

As we come to a close, these tales of those people in our circles seem to be incomplete without my mentioning my father or my girls and our unique relationships.

First, let me just state the weight of a parenting relationship.

A parent's relationship with their child(ren) must be transformational.

Whether the relationship has the term "step" involved in one way or another, or there are certificates that constitute the relationship, this is what we must strive for. As a son of a two transformed parents, they have laid the fundamentals of who I am today. For both my sister and myself, we had the same challenges of two kids growing up, but my parents didn't allow their thoughts on the kind of relationship they wanted with us to change.

Nothing Less

Parents are responsible for so much, including the starting environment for their children's first transitional relationships. We must understand where those environments lead and do our best to mold our kid's minds into ones that are modeled after traits, values, and the God given gifts that He has placed there. We are not entitled to change them, but rather to help harness them and keep them going in the direction to best use them.

When a parental view of a child's relationship is transactional, it establishes a root of constant self-worth that isn't healthy in the long run. "If my child treats me well, I'll treat them well. If my child disrespects me, then I'll disrespect them." That's borderline abuse. If this exists and the view develops in the child, their view of other healthier relationships in transitional or transformational lenses can be distorted by this idea that there needs to be an equal and opposite exchange in order for the relationship to work. As parents we need to know how to *correct* childish behavior but know that the exchange will never be equal. You are their parent, their hero. Showing up is half of the battle we will face in developing a transformational relationship with them.

If the child's relationship is seen more as transitional, the message to the child may be one of "I'm (the parent) just buying time until a better option comes along". We can't see our children as the running list of activities, meals, and bedtimes waiting to be checked off until they leave home someday. Think about it! It can become too easy to develop this mindset when staring down a weekend of soccer tournaments, or house chores that you need attend to and just need to keep the kids busy, or the dreaded school projects are coming up. I can fall into this mindset as many as the other parents I know, and as easy as it can be to look forward to "checking the box" and complete the activity, we are potentially missing an opportunity with those childish eyes watching us go through the motion.

We can't display that for long otherwise another distorted lens covers our children's eyes when looking at potential transformational relationships. These boys and girls need to be the focus, while we dedicate time and energy to maintain the relationship. They may not know it in the moment, but they won't forget it.

Our Capes

Our girls simply call me Jo. We don't ever bother with other terms that go along with my position in their life. Teachers know me as Jo, their friends know me as Jo, it can be that simple. They are my girls. They are not my biological daughters, but that doesn't matter to me. Their biological father plays his role with them during his time, and I play my role when I'm with them.

Whether we are with them or not, we are working every day to expand their world view and expose them to so many more opportunities in the world of which they were previously unaware. Combine this with supporting their growing curiosities, self-discovery of skills and passions, and I have my hands full with how to maintain them. The core time that I dedicate is our Friday morning car rides to school…but more importantly, breakfast on the way to school. That's our zone, that's our time together. Sometimes work calls can be heard over the blue-tooth speakers and Ezra will try to press the unmute button informing the team that I quit. Other times Annorah is in her giggling fit over some of the stories from the week. It's not much, but it's the consistency. This is the reason why I'll do whatever it takes to get home from a client Thursday night, because nothing makes up for our Friday morning commute.

Parenting will be operational for the other hours of the week, but for that 30 minutes, I want to help transform them, to figure out how to be a better champion, how can we develop guardrails for friends, teachers, and bullies. These are my moments, and if I miss them, I might miss the joys of parenting. Stay present.

I get the desire to open the world to my girls because my father was able to do that to me growing up. My father worked from home for a majority of my life (before it was cool) and that was always a hard barrier to understand with him. When was he "working", vs. when could he play. It clicked with me in the later years that for me or my sister, those two sides of the spectrum didn't exist. If he was around, he was Dad, and Dad was ready to transform us however he could. Now it isn't fair to my mom to say that he did it autonomously. Seeing how my wife operates, and just bonding with my mother over parenthood, I discovered that behind every present and focused father is a supportive, instinctive and rather instructive mother helping with the guardrails.

It's hard to keep coming up with additional examples or commentaries for what my parents have taught me on relationships because this entire book is the compilation of all their teachings on the subject.

I've just been fortunate enough to have listed, correlated it to my own personal experiences, prayed that my father and I's words will connect with the readers, and provided the insights that God has led us to communicate to the larger audiences.

CHAPTER 9

Conclusion

What are you going to do about it?"

May we suggest an activity will enhance your experience? Please take a few minutes to answer the following questions and then share them with someone who will hold you accountable.

1. How many relationships do you maintain?

2. Have you ever asked your friends why your friends?

3. Have you ever asked your clients or customers, why they do business with you? Why not?

4. Is there a difference between friends and relationships?

5. Do you have a relationship with your spouse, and do you consider her or him your best friend? Why or why not?

6. How many close friends/relationships do you maintain?

7. Does it bother you to think about these concepts?

When we started this document there was no pandemic. In March of '20, life as we had known it, changed dramatically due to Covid19. We have learned to live in quarantine, learned to follow social distancing, and learned how to make our facemask part of our daily clothing ensemble. This process has led to additional isolation and renewed pressure on all of us to examine and reexamine the relationships we have so highly valued and our ability to interact on a "on demand" basis.

A sign was displayed by residents at a nursing home in our area:
We would rather die of Covid19 than loneliness!

People are living and dying in isolation and Covid19 has dramatically brought worldwide attention to this ongoing syndrome. Initially this book was targeted to help professional salespeople re-engineer themselves in relationship marketing i.e., how to see a relationship differently. Not as the means for a sale or a business goal, but as an opportunity to provide value-added personal service. In this period of isolation, we have realized it's so much more than to be limited to the professional realm, but for the entire life realm.

Years ago, my father adopted from the Bible, Isaiah 50:4 as his business verse when he realized that his calling in the insurance business is just that, a sacred calling:

The Sovereign Lord has given me a well instructed tongue, to know the word that sustains the weary. He wakens me morning by morning, wakens my ear to listen like one being instructed.

Whatever success he has achieved in the "art" of professional selling he owes to the belief and knowledge that God has enabled him to know the word that sustains weary, lonely people whether they were confronted by life, family issues, economic issues, business issues, inflation, Covid19, or relationships! Thank you for investing time and energy in reading this book!

Now to Him who is able to do immeasurably more than all we ask or imagine, according to his power that is at work within us, to Him be the glory in the church and in Christ Jesus throughout all generations, forever and ever! Ephesians 3:20-21

CHAPTER 10

Epilogue- Transfigurational Relationship

Now that we have determined that it is not necessary to live next to a potential client or relationship, nor is it necessary to do something to trade-off for the potential relationship, nor do you need dependence on something or someone to bring you to your next opportunity, where do you go?

That realization is your first step in transformation and subsequent transfiguration. Transformation on the inside becomes transfiguration on the outside. The caterpillar is transformed in the cocoon and released as a transfigured butterfly. Our appearance and self-awareness are forever changed by the supernatural transformation on the inside. Transfiguration is the fulfillment of transformation, *the realization that things will never look the same as they are not the same.* Where do we go for an example? This time we go to the big screen and the 1964 Academy Award Winner for Best Picture "My Fair Lady".

Eliza Doolittle is a Cockney working-class girl who is transformed outwardly to pass as a high society member, and in that process of transformation she is changed inside, transfigured so that her language, her attitude, her being, now reflects from the inside that evidenced on the inside. She becomes outwardly what has happened inwardly!

How does this transfiguration manifest itself in my relationships? Transformation will change our perspectives so that the end no longer justifies the mean, transfiguration will prioritize the end objective for both us and the prospects. That objective ultimately answers the question, how is the development of this relationship in keeping with the commitment we have made to build truth and integrity into all our relationships?

The one negative of Transformational and consequent Transfigurational relationships is that these relationships may grow beyond your purview, and you're forced to let the relationship grow and go. If you try to hang on, you run the risk of destroying that which you have spent years in building and if you let them go too easily you run the risk of their questioning your sincerity and commitment. Personally, we have found that letting go early always makes it easier for them to return should the other relationship not work out. It is all part of a learning experience.

The easiest way that we could explain this transfiguration process that took place in our lives is by utilizing a scripture passage from the Bible, more specifically the book of Romans 12:1-2 (MSG) where the writer, the Apostle Paul says:

"So, here's what I want you to do, God helping you: Take your everyday ordinary life-your sleeping, eating, going-to-work, and walking-around life-and place it before God as an offering.

Embracing what God does for you is the best thing you can do for him. Don't become so well adjusted to your culture that you fit into it without even thinking. Instead, fix your attention on God. You'll be changed from the inside out. Readily recognize what he wants from you, and quickly respond to it. Unlike the culture around you, always dragging you down to its level of immaturity, God brings the best out of you while he develops well- formed maturity in you."

Here's what Paul is saying if you want to permanently change your mind, start by getting your mind right about this world by seeing this world as a platform that can only be changed as you embrace God and his plan for your life, and He develops maturity in you. Only then could I, can you, see relationships and the people that form those relationships as people deserving of God's love and my best. No longer do I see people as transitional or transactional for my own purpose, but I see those people as my opportunity to display God's love for them in mutual respect, kind interactions and extraordinary service. It's amazing the number of people who want to visit with you, want to refer others to you, want you to succeed in whatever opportunity you are pursuing when your desire is to reflect the love of God.

Years ago, my father heard a Pastor talking about decision making and God's will. My father took his advice and applied this truth to relationships. The pastor said that when faced with a difficult decision we should ask ourselves, "How is my decision going to be affected by my lifelong commitment and decision to obey God in all things"? How is this relationship I'm considering in keeping with my decision to honor God in all my relationships?

Since my father started exercising this discipline it has been utterly amazing the "quality" of the new relationships to which he has been exposed and he never lacks the opportunity for more growth both in quality and quantity.

V2

James Johnson is a retired salesmen of 50+ years and a lifelong learner of Relationships. With a passion for people, sales, and teaching, James brings a wealth of knowledge and life experience to this collaboration. After growing up in farmland Minnesota, James has lived at the tip of Lake Superior for 30+ years with his wife (Peg) and raised two children (Lizi and Josiah) in the beauty of Duluth. Beyond writing, he enjoys reading, teaching and learning at local bible studies, traveling with friends, following Minnesota Sports, and spending time with his grandchildren.

Josiah Johnson is an engineer turned business consultant and recognized data nerd. Some are surprised that Josiah's first book wasn't around data or excel reports, but driven by a shared love of relationship dynamics with his father, Josiah contributed a fresh perspective to this book, blending tradition with modern insights. In his free time, he enjoys traveling with his Wife (Grethell) and Ezra and Annorah, along with golfing, woodworking and data-modeling.

Together, James and Josiah have created this book as a labor of love, capturing the wisdom, humor, and curiosity that have bonded them as both family and collaborators. They hope their work brings joy, inspiration, and thought-provoking moments to readers of all ages. Their natural partnership comes from a life-long career thesis that James has been working to share, along with Josiah's passion for writing and teaching management teams on core business concepts as well as professional and personal relationships.